Sharpened, Wielded, & Ready

A 70-Day Devotional From My Journey Into TRUTH

F. D. Adkins

F. D. Adkins LLC

Contents

Preface 3

1. And So My Journey Began... 7

2. Hold On Tight 10

3. So Many Questions??? 13

4. Six Days 16

5. Mr. Right 20

6. What Will I Wear Today? 23

7. Grateful or Hateful? 26

8. An Unexpected Guest 29

9. Under HIS Shadow 32

10. Game Plan 35

11.	Turn On the Light	39
12.	Hear His Voice	42
13.	No Internet Connection Required	45
14.	How Can I Be Strong?	48
15.	Free To Fly	50
16.	I Cry... And He Hears	53
17.	Weeds	57
18.	Through the Eyes of a Child	62
19.	Coordinates (X, Why?)	66
20.	Need Directions?	70
21.	Warrior Sisters	73
22.	Adjusting the Thermostat	76
23.	Paid In Full	80
24.	Always A Purpose for the Season	85
25.	A Reflection of Truth	88
26.	The Good Fruit	91
27.	Only By His Power	94
28.	Heart Transplant	98
29.	Eyes on Jesus	103
30.	Letting Go	106

31. The Power of the Sword   110

32. No Room for Compromise   112

33. Look At the Map   115

34. Emotional Waves   119

35. Two Out Of Twelve   123

36. Don't Let the Sun Go Down   126

37. Through the Tears   131

38. Molt and Move Forward   134

39. No X-Ray Needed   137

40. The TRUTH Is Still There   139

41. Yearn to Learn   142

42. Faith That Holds   145

43. It Wasn't Me   148

44. Do Others See Jesus in Me?   151

45. The ONE Who Understands   154

46. Stand Out   158

47. Rich Without Measure   161

48. A Safe Haven   165

49. When You Know it's from God   168

50. Strong Enough to be Meek   172

51. It May Storm... But the Son Is Always There   175

52. The World May Be Changing... BUT...   179

53. I Didn't Ask   184

54. Tunnel Vision   189

55. A Cry for Help   193

56. Breaking Point   197

57. He Never Knew the Easy Life   202

58. When the Enemy Attacks   206

59. Surrounded   210

60. It's In the Perspective   213

61. Discerning the Truth   218

62. This is the Day   221

63. The Richest Man   224

64. The Good Soil   228

65. Hopeless? Never!   233

66. One Step at a Time   236

67. What's on the Menu?   240

68. Our Only Shelter   243

69. It's Beyond Me   246

70. The Next Rainbow   249

Notes   255

Sharpening Our Sword   259

Acknowledgements   268

About the Author   269

To my Heavenly Father,
For never forsaking me on my journey,
For giving me a nudge when I am afraid to step in faith,
And for reminding me of the TRUTH in the words I so often recite,
"I can do all things through Christ which strengtheneth me."
Philippians 4:13 KJV

To my wonderful husband,
For cheering me on when I succeed,
For picking up me when I fail,
And not letting me quit.
For all the sacrifices you have made
to support our family,
But most of all,
For always loving me.

To my amazing children,
For believing in your mom and being excited about my books,
For allowing me to share some of your stories,
For being my technological guides,
But especially for being the greatest children a mother could hope for.
I am so proud of the young adults you have become, and I pray you
will always keep God with you on your journey.

To my mother,
For proofreading when you don't feel like it,
For reassuring me when I doubt myself,
For being my mom and not just my mother.
But above all, being there when I need you.

To my warrior sister,
For never missing one of my posts,
For your dedicated texts of encouragement each morning,
For helping me hold my shield when it becomes too heavy and standing
with me in battle.
For being the friend who sharpens me.

Preface

Twenty-one years ago, my husband and I decided to have children. With that decision, we stepped out on faith, and I left my job to be a full-time wife and mother. Adapting a budget from two incomes to one is not easy. But we lived within our means, and God always provided. When my two children hit their teen years, I felt God calling me to do something more. I knew I still wanted to be home and available for my children full-time, yet I could not deny this tugging at my heart.

For months, I prayed over this weight pressing on my soul, unsure of what on earth I was supposed to do. I had not worked in years. I only had a two-year degree and could not think of one talent that stood out that could be of use.

Then one morning, out of the blue, an idea popped into my head for a Christian suspense novel. I loved to read and had discovered the Christian fiction genre a few years before. I was amazed that I could enjoy an action-packed mystery that was not only clean but also contained a message of faith.

I began writing in my spare time, never actually expecting to finish it, but a year later, I did. Friends and family encouraged me to submit it to publishers. I was skeptical, especially after reading articles about what publishers like to see in a book proposal. I had no network or connections in the writing industry and no website or social following (I was not on social media at all). However, I did not want to self-publish my first book. If my novel was going to be published, I needed to know that it was because someone in the field thought it was good enough. After all, I had no writing experience.

I created my own website and began posting to a weekly blog. I opened a social media account and continued to play around with editing my novel. In an effort to gain some experience, I submitted a freelance article to a well-known Christian magazine. A couple of months passed by, along with my recollection of the article. In the meantime, I had signed up for a local writing conference that just happened to be hosted by some of my favorite authors. However, as the conference drew near, I became anxious and thought of backing out. I was sure that I would not and could not fit in with all of these seasoned and educated writers.

But then God stepped in and gave me a nudge. The day before the conference, I received an email from the Christian magazine wanting to purchase my article. I went to that conference, and I fit in just fine. I learned a lot... and come to find out... one of those favorite authors I was excited to see... said she had no education in writing either. She started as a stay-at-home mother. (I felt that was another nudge from God).

In short, I submitted that first book to a few publishers, and within a couple of months, I received a contract. I now have three Christian Suspense novels and a few published freelance articles. But the message here is... "FOR WITH GOD NOTHING SHALL BE IMPOSSIBLE," Luke 1:37 KJV.

I am not an expert on the Bible. I am a sinner saved by Grace. I am a work in progress aspiring to grow closer to my Savior and deepen my relationship with Him every day. I am an introvert who feels awkward in social situations, yet a slow and lulling ache in my chest keeps pushing me to share what is in my heart.

So, here goes. This devotional is made up of thoughts, stories, and personal experiences that have come to mind throughout my own journey into TRUTH. Simply put, the following contains the messages that have weighed on my soul as I read God's Word. I compare studying my Bible to sharpening my sword. The more I study and search God's Word, the more equipped I am to use the scripture as an offensive and defensive weapon in the daily battle against the enemy. I hope you enjoy reading, but most of all, I hope this book encourages you in your walk with Christ.

And So My Journey Began...

"BEHOLD, I STAND AT THE DOOR AND KNOCK: IF ANY MAN HEAR MY VOICE, AND OPEN THE DOOR, I WILL COME IN TO HIM, AND WILL SUP WITH HIM, AND HE WITH ME." REVELATION 3:20 KJV

And so my journey began....

When I designed my website with the intent of writing a weekly blog, I knew the purpose was to share what God had placed on my heart through my own study of His Word. After all, the penning of my novels had begun with the goal of sharing my faith through my writing, so I had no doubts that this was where He was leading me. Yet, at the same time, I had no idea of the magnitude to which this new quest would affect me.

Upon the initial launch of my blog page, I wanted each post to be personal, conveying the message that I had received from a particular scripture or study. In doing so, I found myself digging into God's Word like never before. Instead of reading a few verses or a chapter, I needed to confirm every message in its entirety. The more I read, the hungrier I became yearning to learn more. My desire for Truth was insatiable.

In many of my posts and the pages that follow, I have disclosed my obsessive-compulsive nature. I was diagnosed with OCD around the age of twelve. That said, a regular daily routine easily takes root. But as I embarked on my new journey, studying God's Word in this new way, I came to a soul-shaking realization. Up until this point, I had been keeping a morning appointment with God. And yes, time with God should be the number one priority on my schedule... but not just as an appointment. God wants a relationship with me. Revelation 3:20 says, "Behold, I stand at the door and knock: if any man hear my voice, and open the door, I will come in to him, and will sup with him, and he with me" (KJV). The first thing I note from this verse is that Jesus does not wait for us to come to Him. He comes to us. He knocks on our door asking to come in. Second, when we let Him in, He wants to spend time with us. As in sharing a meal, He wants personal one-on-one, quality time. When I have coffee or dinner with someone, I spend time talking and listening. This is what my Heavenly Father desires with me.

Reading our Bibles and spending time in prayer are not daily assignments. If the love of our lives knocks on the door, we are not going to pencil a date in on the calendar. Our hearts will burn with a desire to spend every minute with that person. But wait... the love of our lives is knocking at the door. His unconditional love for us is etched in the scars on His hands. Let's have dinner with Jesus. Let's spend time building and strengthening the relationship that is guaranteed to last forever.

BIBLE READING: REVELATION 3:20

Hold On Tight

"THERE ARE MANY DEVICES IN A MAN'S HEART; NEVERTHELESS THE COUNSEL OF THE LORD, THAT SHALL STAND." PROVERBS 19:21 KJV

One minute, life has us high in the treetops, basking in the sun, and dancing from limb to limb to a beautiful concert of the birds singing around us. And then, a second later, the tree goes crashing to the ground, and we are left barely hanging on.

I memorized Philippians 4:6-7 a while ago, and now, I recite these verses over and over to myself on a daily basis. These verses instruct, "Be careful for nothing; but in every thing by prayer and supplication with thanksgiving let your requests be made known unto God. And the peace of God, which passeth all understanding, shall keep your hearts and minds through Christ Jesus" (KJV).

Worry is one of my major weaknesses. I have wasted so much time in past years worrying about things out of my control and things that never happen. However, the enemy knows worry can paralyze me, so if he can plant a thought that will keep my mind cycling with 'what ifs,' I will not accomplish what God has set for me to do that day.

Recently, I admit worry tried to get the best of me. I allowed one of those 'what if' scenarios to control my thoughts. Even though I had been reciting the words to these verses, apparently the 'Be careful for nothing' part was not sinking in because I found myself filled with anxiety and crumbling from exhaustion. Yet, in the midst of my worrying fit, God sent me a message. How? I'm not talking about a roaring voice or a letter dropping from the sky. But this message was no doubt from God.

See, as I sat trembling, my knees knocking with worry, I received a text from a friend. Note that I had not communicated with this friend in a few days, so she did not know of my anxiety and this new worry, especially to the extent that my panic had escalated at that very moment. However, when I picked up my phone and clicked on her text, she had not typed a message. Instead, she had sent a beautiful picture of a landscape, and in the center of the landscape printed in bold letters were the words, "Don't worry. God is in control." Considering the impeccable timing, her lack of knowledge concerning my stress level at that instant, and the exact words I needed to hear right then, I do not doubt that God had used my friend to send me a reminder.

At that moment, Philippians 4:6-7 flooded into my mind. I needed to go to God with thanksgiving and let Him worry for me. Without pause, I got on my knees.

Most of my worries carry no real weight, yet they can feel so backbreakingly heavy. Sometimes, the world brings about anxiety and stress that seems too much to bear. But God is in control, and if we trust Him completely, we do not have to carry it alone. The Israelites thought they were finished when they arrived at the edge of the sea with nowhere else to go. But God parted the waters. Elijah had no desire to live anymore. Of course, God knew his real need was food and rest, and He provided. The disciples thought Jesus was dead, but He had risen. Jesus paid the price and overcame death so that we could have eternal life.

God is in control. He has a plan... and His plan prevails. Always!

BIBLE READING: PHILIPPIANS 4; PROVERBS 19:21

So Many Questions???

"FOR MY THOUGHTS ARE NOT YOUR THOUGHTS, NEITHER ARE YOUR WAYS MY WAYS, SAITH THE LORD. FOR AS THE HEAVENS ARE HIGHER THAN THE EARTH, SO ARE MY WAYS HIGHER THAN YOUR

WAYS, AND MY THOUGHTS THAN YOUR THOUGHTS." ISAIAH 55:8-9 KJV

When I was a child, I was diagnosed with obsessive-compulsive disorder. Cycling thoughts brought relentless worry and many sleepless nights, and repetitive hand washing often left my hands cracked and bleeding. And I must admit, sometimes I wondered why... why did I have to suffer... why could I not control my thoughts... and stop washing my hands? I know it sounds like one should be able to stop, but with OCD, it's not quite that simple.

Of course, now that I look back on that struggle, I know it did not go without purpose. On those worrisome nights, I came to know and grew closer to God. In addition, those bouts of worry prepared me and gave me the strength to endure the greater worries that come with adult life.

In the book of Job, we read about a man faithful to God, yet this man suffered great loss and pain. In the midst of his troubles, Job did not understand that it was Satan causing this pain and suffering. Job believed he was being punished unjustly by God, and Job had questions. In Job 31:35, Job exclaims, "Oh that one would hear me! Behold, my desire is, that the Almighty would answer me, and that mine adversary had written a book" (KJV).

Sometimes, it is difficult to understand and accept why things happen (or don't happen). Sometimes, our human brains, fueled by our emotions, want answers. Sometimes, we have so many questions.

Maybe, God does not answer a prayer in the way we want. Perhaps, God is saying wait when we think he isn't hearing us at all, or maybe our request does not align with what He knows is best. After all, He does know the future, and we do not. Yet, our human nature is impatient, and especially in today's age where technology makes us wait for nothing, we expect answers now.

Paul addresses those questions that we have in 1 Corinthians 13:12 as he writes, "For now we see through a glass, darkly; but then face to face: now I know in part; but then shall I know even as also I am known" (KJV). While we are on this earth, we may not have all the answers, but one day when we meet our SAVIOR face to face, we will understand. God knows all, and one day we will understand ourselves and know ourselves as God does.

For now, we must cling to TRUTH and trust our SAVIOR until that day when we meet HIM face to face.

Let us not forget God's words in Isaiah 55:8-9, "For my thoughts are not your thoughts, neither are your ways my ways, saith the Lord. For as the heavens are higher than the earth, so are my ways higher than your ways, and my thoughts than your thoughts" (KJV).

BIBLE READING: JOB 31; ISAIAH 55:8-9; 1 CORINTHIANS 13:12

Six Days

"SIX DAYS SHALT THOU LABOUR, AND DO ALL THY WORK." EXODUS 20:9 KJV

Night after night, week after week, he stares at the screen thinking, drawing, and calculating the elevation of the land, the foundation, the cost of building materials, and a floor plan without wasted space. In his mind, every board, every nail, and every brick is carefully placed.

After mapping the path to save the most, he gazes up at the first to go. He analyzes the natural lean and asks himself, "Which way should it fall?" He yanks the starter cord, and the roar of the saw fills the woods. A careful notch and then a cut sends the tree whistling through the air to collide with the earth. One down, but he does not count how many more. He just moves to the next and then the next. He makes a seven-hundred-fifty-foot driveway and a seat for our home, falling one tree at a time. If only it were as simple as cutting trees. Now tree stumps dot the path. With a little backhoe attachment on his tractor, he tackles the dotted path stump by stump.

Once the route to the house seat is complete, he is ready to start bringing those plans to life. Tiny scoop by tiny scoop, he uses that same tractor with that same little backhoe attachment to dig a full basement and footers. Foundation walls go up, and then he sets the floor trusses. In a one-man show, he climbs the ladder and lays one end of the floor truss on the wall. Moving to the other side, he climbs the ladder and lifts the other side of the truss. One down, he moves to the next. Flooring, walls, more trusses, more walls, and a roof, he builds board by board, nail by nail. What is usually done with multiple crews of men, he does all by himself.

Maybe this sounds a little far-fetched. Maybe this even sounds impossible. But I have witnessed this one-man show, and I have pictures to prove it.

I share this story because this man is my inspiration. He has taught me that if one wants something, one has to work for it, and anything worth having requires hard work. I have been married to him for twenty-five years, and this is the third house he has built. His motivation and perseverance have saved the money that allowed me to quit work and stay home to raise our children. Most people would probably view one person building a whole house as impossible, but the Bible tells us that nothing is impossible with God.

Projects used to overwhelm me because I would look at the entire feat and get discouraged. As I have watched my husband over the years, I have learned to climb a mountain one step at a time. It takes more than one step to get to the top of Mount Everest. My husband did not focus on plumbing and electrical before he built the walls. He did not worry about brick before he dug a basement. He took it one phase at a time.

God even gives us this example to follow. God is all-powerful and could easily have created everything in the blink of an eye. But instead, He took creation day by day. In addition, the Bible also commands us to work. One of the commandments is to keep the Sabbath by not working on that day. However, we are called to work on the other six. In Exodus 20:9-10, God commands, "Six days shalt thou labour, and do all thy work: But the seventh day is the sabbath of the Lord thy God: in it thou shalt not do any work..."(KJV).

BIBLE READING: EXODUS 20:9-10; GENESIS 1

Mr. Right

"BUT WHOSOEVER DRINKETH OF THE WATER THAT I SHALL GIVE HIM SHALL NEVER THIRST; BUT THE WATER THAT I SHALL GIVE HIM SHALL BE IN HIM A WELL OF WATER SPRINGING UP INTO EVERLASTING LIFE." JOHN 4:14 KJV

She had been searching for Mr. Right. The void in her heart must have been yearning desperately to be filled. Here she was after five attempts at marriage and a man she had never wed, and she was walking to the well... alone... all by herself. As she approached the well, she had no idea she was about to meet the One, the only ONE whose love could fill the void.

In the trek of life, the desire for happiness sometimes takes us on this wild chase. We often perceive that we will finally be satisfied if we can make more money... if we can afford our dream home... if we can meet the perfect spouse to share our lives with... if we can land the ideal job... if we can find fame in the eyes of the world... if... if... if... if we can just have or accomplish these things, the void inside us would finally be filled.

But is it ever filled? Are we ever satisfied with any of these things?

The enemy loves to dangle shiny objects in front of us, just as he tempted Eve with the apple. James 1:14 states, "But every man is tempted, when he is drawn away of his own lust, and enticed" (KJV), and 1 Peter 5:8 warns, "... your adversary the devil, as a roaring lion, walketh about, seeking whom he may devour" (KJV). If he distracts us with worldly desires, he keeps us veering off and away from the path that leads to the only One who can truly fill that void.

John, chapter four, tells the story of a woman who had been married five times and was in a relationship with a man she had not wed, yet she was walking alone. But when she arrived at the well, she found that she was not alone. Jesus was there waiting for her.

Friends, we are not alone. We have no need to search. Jesus is there waiting.

BIBLE READING: JOHN 4; JAMES 1:14; 1 PETER 5:8

What Will I Wear Today?

"FOR WE WRESTLE NOT AGAINST FLESH AND BLOOD, BUT AGAINST PRINCIPALITIES, AGAINST POWERS, AGAINST THE RULERS OF THE DARKNESS OF THIS WORLD, AGAINST SPIRITUAL WICKEDNESS IN HIGH PLACES."
EPHESIANS 6:12 KJV

N ow that I am older, I put a bit more thought into making sure that I am dressed for whatever elements I might encounter in the place where I am going. For example, if it is cold outside and I am going to a ballgame, I will wear multiple layers. I've even been known to wear snow pants for the insulation, even though it is not snowing. If I go to the beach, I wear plenty of sunscreen. My comfort overshadows my appearance. I do not want to be cold, nor do I want to endure the pain of a sunburn for days. If I am prepared and wearing the right protective gear, I will not be bothered by things that could cause discomfort.

In Ephesians 6:13-17, Paul details each piece of our spiritual armor. Why would we need spiritual armor? In Ephesians 6:11, Paul tells us, "Put on the whole armour of God, that ye may be able to stand against the wiles of the devil," and a couple of verses later in Ephesians 6:13, he reiterates, "Wherefore take unto you the whole armour of God, that ye may be able to withstand in the evil day, and having done all, to stand" (KJV).

As I read these verses a few weeks ago, the words, "...having done all...," stood out to me as if they were written in bold letters, and this sudden epiphany exploded inside my head. If I do not consciously put on every piece of the armor of God every day, then I am not doing 'all' to prepare myself for the enemy's attacks. I would not go out into a blizzard in snow pants and a tank top. I would need a winter coat, proper boots, a hat, insulated gloves, and maybe even a face covering. In the same way, why would I start my day knowing the devil will try to attack with only my shield or my helmet? Every piece has a purpose, and I need to suit up with all of them.

So, first thing each morning, I hope you will join me in making every effort to put on the whole armor of God so that we are doing 'all' to protect ourselves from the enemy because we know the battle is real. Let us buckle on the belt of TRUTH, wrapping ourselves in God's Word and knowing we have accepted Jesus as our Savior. Let us cover our hearts with the breastplate of righteousness, adhering to God's Word. Let us slip our feet into the shoes of peace, standing with our feet firmly planted on the hope that comes only with a personal relationship with Jesus. Let us protect our minds with our helmet of salvation, keeping our thoughts and focus on Christ. Let us extinguish the devil's lies by lifting our shield of faith in front of us. And let us pick up our sword of the Spirit, not only reading but also memorizing scripture.

After all, what soldier would go into battle without the proper gear and protection?

Bible Reading: Ephesians 6:10-20

Grateful or Hateful?

"... FOR I HAVE LEARNED, IN WHATSOEVER STATE I AM, THEREWITH TO BE CONTENT."
PHILIPPIANS 4:11 KJV

Surrounded by a paradise of plenty, Eve's thoughts turned to the one thing she could not have.

A rescue from slavery, an escape on dry land through the middle of a sea, and daily bread delivered to their doorstep each morning were all forgotten in the blink of an eye. At the first sign of difficulty, the Israelites would turn from grateful to hateful.

Paul, after being beaten, sang praises to God as he sat chained in a prison cell. Paul also wrote these words while imprisoned. *"Rejoice in the Lord always: and again I say, Rejoice. ...for I have learned, in whatsoever state I am, therewith to be content. I know both how to be abased, and I know how to abound: every where and in all things I am instructed both to be full and to be hungry, both to abound and to suffer need" (Philippians 4:4, 11-12 KJV).*

So, I ask myself, "Which of these characterizations best describes me?" Am I thankful in the hard times, or do I grumble at the least little stumble?

In the middle of a storm that leaves a trail of broken branches, it is not always easy to have a sincere and grateful heart. Yet, Paul, who must have been in severe pain after having been beaten, sang praises. How is it possible to have this kind of gratitude... to keep this kind of mindset in the midst of hardship? Paul explains in Philippians 4:8 (KJV), "...whatsoever things are true, whatsoever things are honest, whatsoever things are just, whatsoever things are pure, whatsoever things are lovely, whatsoever things are of good report; if there be any virtue, and if there be any praise, think on these things."

Eve's focus drifted from the bounty of blessings around her to one tree she was not supposed to eat of. Fruit galore was there for her taking, but she failed to ponder on that.

The Israelites seemed to have a continuous battle with amnesia. Despite the many miracles God had performed to save them, they had tunnel vision when it came to their comfort.

Yet, Paul said in Philippians 1:21, "For to me to live is Christ, and to die is gain" (KJV). Paul's eyes were on the finish line.

Each day, we have a choice. We can choose to be grateful, or we can choose to be hateful. We can choose to forget what God has done and whine about the present situation... OR... we can choose to remember all that God has given. If we choose to think of the cross and the unconditional love of a Savior who suffered and died to save us from eternal torment, how can we not be grateful?

BIBLE READING: PHILIPPIANS 1; PHILIPPIANS 4:8-13

An Unexpected Guest

"Watch therefore: for ye know not what hour your Lord doth come."
Matthew 24:42 KJV

I t was a Saturday morning, and my husband had already left to go and work on the new house we were building. As usual, before heading over, I finished getting ready and stopped at the gas station for coffee and biscuits. As I pulled up the drive, my husband stood on the ladder by the garage door, installing the wiring for our outside lights. I loaded my arms with our coffee cups, my water, a coke, and a biscuit, and somewhere in the midst of all that, I tucked my phone under my arm. As I ambled toward the house where my husband was working, he motioned toward the woods. I looked over, and a white turkey was strutting out of the trees. Desperately, I tried to get my phone to take a picture, but with all the stuff in my hands, I was stuck. I stood frozen for a second with my mind whirring. I was afraid to make any abrupt movements. I didn't want to scare the turkey away. Finally, in the slowest of motions, I squatted, put all my stuff on the ground, and slipped the phone from beneath my arm. I snapped several pictures. Amazingly, the turkey kept strutting toward us and went right up to the bottom of the ladder my husband was standing on. Seemingly comfortable with his environment, the turkey almost nodded off to sleep once and eventually laid down. I got quite a few photos and even a video before he disappeared back into the woods.

Later that day, I was thinking about that turkey. I had never seen a white turkey in the wild before and certainly would never have expected one to come walking out of our woods. As much as I love taking photos of nature, especially animals, if I had expected it, I would not have had my arms full. I would have been readily waiting with my camera in my hand.

However, God's Word tells me that Jesus is coming back. I do not know when, but I should expect His return and be ready at any moment. In Luke 12:40, Jesus warns, "Be ye therefore ready also: for the Son of man cometh at an hour when ye think not" (KJV). Those words are affirmed in 1 Thessalonians

5:2, "For yourselves know perfectly that the day of the Lord so cometh as a thief in the night" (KJV).

What will happen if we are not ready (or in my example if our hands are too full)?

Jesus says that on that day, "Then shall two be in the field; the one shall be taken, and the other left. Two women shall be grinding at the mill; the one shall be taken, and the other left" (Matthew 24:40-41 KJV).

Jesus is coming back. And when He does, let's be sure that our hands aren't full of the things of this world. Let's have our eyes on Heaven, watching and ready for Him to take us home. When that moment comes, there won't be a second chance to empty our hands.

Bible Reading: Matthew 24:21-42; Luke 12:40; 1 Thessalonians 5:2

Under HIS Shadow

"He that dwelleth in the secret place of the Most High shall abide under the shadow of the Almighty. I will say of the Lord, He is my refuge and my fortress: my God; in Him will I trust." Psalm 91:1-2 KJV

The other morning, I woke up to a steady rain that continued most of the day. As I worked in the kitchen, I noticed a cat curled up on the couch on our back porch. I walked over and looked at it through the French door window. For a brief moment, it peered back at me, then stretched out and went to sleep. I had no idea who the cat belonged to, but at the time, it seemed to need a dry place to rest. The cat slept for several hours, and then, when the rain stopped, it stepped off the porch and disappeared into the woods. The thick trees behind our house are home to many animals, most of which we never know are there because God has gifted each of them their own way of blending in to stay safe. In addition, the trees shelter them from the heavy rain and give them shade from the heat. The forest is their refuge.

A while back, I chose to commit Psalm 91:1-2 to memory. The strange thing is, when I chose these verses to memorize, I did not realize how much these words would help me get through the following week. That said, I am sure it was no coincidence that I chose that specific scripture to memorize at that specific time. Friends, we all need a refuge, a place to curl up, feel safe, and know we are not alone. I am not talking about a physical structure. I am referring to a place where our hearts and souls are at peace, where we feel joy despite the circumstances, where we lift our hands and let go of the worry. As I knelt in prayer that week when the darkness seemed to be closing in around me, I found myself letting the words of Psalm 91:1 wash over me. And then, I repeated Psalm 91:2 aloud claiming its Truth. "...He is my refuge and my fortress: my God; in Him will I trust" (Psalm 91:2 KJV).

How great is the peace and assurance that comes from knowing we are under the shadow of the Almighty! What a blessing to know that under His shadow, we can rest safe and secure!

Our circumstances during this life will constantly change, and the valleys may outnumber the mountaintops. But if we know Christ, we can find rest and joy in the refuge of our God, having the assurance that this life is only a temporary stop because the battle has already been won. Our permanent mountaintop awaits.

Let's arm ourselves with His Truth. Let's claim the words together...,

"I will say of the Lord, He is my refuge and my fortress: my God; in Him will I trust." Psalm 91:2 KJV

BIBLE READING: PSALM 91

Game Plan

"FOR THE WORD OF GOD IS QUICK, AND POWERFUL, AND SHARPER THAN ANY TWOEDGED SWORD, PIERCING EVEN TO THE DIVIDING ASUNDER OF SOUL AND

SPIRIT, AND OF THE JOINTS AND MARROW, AND IS A DISCERNER OF THE THOUGHTS

AND INTENTS OF THE HEART." HEBREWS 4:12 KJV

As the teams are chosen, the battle is on, and I can't help but laugh. We have played just about every sport as a family in the backyard, and no matter the sport, whoever is paired with me is certain to lose. Why? Because I cannot throw a ball, catch a ball, or hit a ball with a bat or a club, nor do I seem to have any reflexes or speedy reaction time. Running is the extent of my athletic ability. So, as we stand in the backyard, my son, daughter, and husband try to decide who will get stuck with Mom.

For today's football game, my husband is the lucky one. He pulls me to the side, giving me the fine details of the play. I am supposed to run left, then back right, then left again, and that is when he will throw me the ball.

I lift my eyebrows with a blank stare.

"What?" he asks as if the plan he has just mapped out should be easy-peasy.

I lean in. "I just don't see the point in all of the running back and forth when we both know I am not going to catch the ball."

"Okay," he drops his gaze, "would you rather throw the ball?"

I shake my head. "No, I can't do that either."

"Then, what do you suggest?"

I crack a smile. "Hand me the ball, and I will run."

It works for the first play. The kids don't expect me not to go out for a pass. I have made it past them before they realize I already have the ball, and I score a touchdown. It even works a second time. But then they catch on, and both have me tagged the second I have the ball in my hands.

As we were sitting at a high school tennis match the other night, I noticed how one of the players was hitting the same shot down the line over and over. I began to think about how athletes strategize and form a game plan to outwit their opponent by watching past games, searching for any visible strengths or weaknesses or repetitious moves (in the same way that my kids picked up on my repetitive play in football).

From there, I pondered the opponent I face every day... the one who whispers in my ear that I'm not good enough... the one who tells me I'll never be enough... the one who gets me so focused on my to-do list that I lose sight of the blessings around me... the one who distracts me with the past, so I won't press on toward the finish line.

By studying the Bible, we know how the enemy works. Just as he made Eve focus on the one tree that she was not supposed to eat of instead of the plethora of other trees around her, he wants to magnify our wants and blind us to the things God has given us. When he whispers in our ears, we know he is "...a liar, and the father of it" (John 8:44 KJV). When we are on that mountaintop and then suddenly find ourselves crumpled in the valley, we know our "...adversary the devil, as a roaring lion, walketh about, seeking whom he may devour" (1 Peter 5:8 KJV). And we know that our enemy likes to wear disguises and try to deceive us, "... for Satan himself is transformed into an angel of light" (2 Corinthians 11:14 KJV).

If we know how the enemy works, we can be on the offense. Before he whispers I am not good enough, I can lift my hands in praise, reciting Psalm 139:14, "I will praise thee; for I am fearfully and wonderfully made: marvellous are thy works; and that my soul knoweth right well" (KJV). Instead of letting him blind me to my blessings, I can fall to my knees each morning and "In every thing give thanks..." (1 Thessalonians 5:18 KJV). When I find myself lying in the valley, I can be assured that I am not alone because God's Word tells me, "...Be strong and of a good courage; be not afraid, neither be thou dismayed: for the Lord thy God is with thee whithersoever thou goest" (Joshua 1:9 KJV).

Today, we will be attacked. But we know the enemy's tactics, and we know the TRUTH. Let's play offense. Let's stay armed with the TRUTH.

BIBLE READING: HEBREWS 4:12; JOHN 8:44; 1 PETER 5:7; 2 CORINTHIANS 11:14; PSALM 139:14; 1 THESSALONIANS 5:18; JOSHUA 1:9

Turn On the Light

"THY WORD IS A LAMP UNTO MY FEET, AND
A LIGHT UNTO MY PATH." PSALM 119:105
KJV

When my husband and I were building our house, we were there working almost every evening. However, one evening, in particular, we had stayed a bit later, so it was darker than usual as I walked to my car. Dense clouds filled the sky, concealing the light from the moon and the stars, but since I always followed that same path to my car, I didn't think much of the darkness or even bother using the flashlight on my phone. I just trudged along, and knowing myself, I am guessing my mind was a million miles away, thinking about what I needed to do when I got home or brainstorming the next scene in my book. But, when I started my car and flipped on my headlights, I was shocked. *I was surrounded and didn't even know it.* Deer were everywhere, standing all in the driveway in front of my car and as far as I could see into the woods. Now, I love animals, so even though I know those woods are full of deer, and I see them all the time, I was still excited and tried to take pictures. However, the point is that I was not aware that the deer were all around me as I walked to the car because I didn't use my flashlight.

And then recently, I picked up one of those expensive college textbooks from the shelf I had purchased for one of my kid's classes. Since that class had long passed, I decided to sell it. As I knocked the dust from the book, I realized that this book had never been opened, or for that matter, even moved from that spot since it came in the mail. I couldn't help but think how much more could have been learned in that course had the book actually been utilized.

Psalm 119:105 says, "Thy word is a lamp unto my feet, and a light unto my path" (KJV), and Paul warns of the battle we fight in this dark world as he states, "For we wrestle not against flesh and blood, but against principalities, against powers, against the rulers of the darkness of this world, against spiritual wickedness in high places" (Ephesians 6:12 KJV).

How do I fight against the darkness of this world? I need the light. I need God's Word to guide me through the darkness and illuminate the right path. However, in order for the light to come on, I have to open my Bible, cling to the Truth inside, and keep its words in my heart.

Let's not forget to turn on the light... and keep it on every day.

BIBLE READING: PSALM 119:105; EPHESIANS 6:12

Hear His Voice

"MY SHEEP HEAR MY VOICE, AND I KNOW THEM, AND THEY FOLLOW ME: AND I GIVE UNTO THEM ETERNAL LIFE; AND THEY SHALL NEVER PERISH, NEITHER SHALL ANY MAN PLUCK THEM OUT OF MY HAND."
JOHN 10:27-28 KJV

I had previously heard somewhere that a baby could start to recognize voices in the womb. Now, to be clear, I am not an expert on the matter, nor have I researched the evidence to back up the theory. But during my pregnancies, I talked, sang, and even read books to my children. With my first child, I had a rather long commute to work, so he got a full concert during my route which included the song, "Jesus Loves Me," many times over. Later on, at the hospital a couple of days after he was born, my husband and I discovered that when my son cried, if I would sing "Jesus Loves Me," he would stop crying and listen.

In the Gospel of John 10:27-28, Jesus says, "My sheep hear my voice, and I know them and they follow me: And I give unto them eternal life; and they shall never perish, neither shall any man pluck them out of my hand." (KJV)

In John chapter ten, the Jews surround Jesus and question Him, asking if He is the Christ. Jesus responds by not only detailing that He has already told them, but that the miracles and works He has done in His Father's Name are evidence. He then continues by explaining that because they choose not to believe, they do not listen. And because they do not hear Him, they are not His sheep.

"But ye believe not, because ye are not of my sheep, as I said unto you." John 10:26 KJV

It is often said that the older we get, the more we get stuck in our ways. And I have to admit that I frequently see that in myself. I make my bed as soon as I get out of it, and it would trouble me to no end to walk out of my bedroom without doing it. E-books may be cheaper, but I grew up holding a paper copy in my hand. The only way I read an e-book is if the paper copy is unavailable or a tremendous difference in price forces it. In school, I learned there were nine planets. It does not matter that our children are taught there are only eight. If someone asks, I will still probably note that Pluto is a planet.

The Jews addressing Jesus in this chapter of John did not want to believe that Jesus was the Messiah. They did not want to open their ears to Jesus' words or take in the evidence of His works.

On the contrary, Jesus' sheep hear His voice, and He knows them, and they follow Him. (John 10:27 KJV).

If we belong to Christ... if we have sincerely invited Him into our hearts... if we are one of His sheep, we may endure trials and tribulations and the enemy may try to trip us up on every corner... But be assured that NO ONE or NOTHING can take us from the hands of our Savior.

"... neither shall any man pluck them out of my hand." John 10:28 KJV

BIBLE READING: JOHN 10

No Internet Connection Required

"PRAY WITHOUT CEASING." 1 THESSALONIANS 5:17 KJV

In today's world, we have become quite dependent on our access to the web. A while back, we were having issues with our internet service. The signal was intermittent. One minute we had service, and the next minute we didn't, which made it difficult to accomplish any work that required a strong connection. And of course, my son had procrastinated taking his final exam for his online course. Thankfully, it came back on long enough for him to get it completed. However, when my daughter tried to write her essay, she finally had to give up and go to the neighbor's house.

Meanwhile, I was making a plan for the day since I had to work around the appointment for the technician to repair our internet, and a sudden thought struck me. *What a blessing that our prayer line to God never goes out.* I can talk to God anytime and anywhere, and no internet connection is required. And, I can't imagine trying to get through the day without having my Heavenly Father to talk to. I have so much to tell him about and discuss with Him, and summarizing my thoughts is not my strong suit (hence, one of the reasons I write novels instead of short stories).

When does the Bible say to pray? Here are a few verses that answer that question. (Note the underlined words.)

- "Rejoicing in hope; patient in tribulation; **continuing** instant in prayer." Romans 12:12 KJV

- "Pray **without ceasing**." 1 Thessalonians 5:17 KJV

- "**Continue** in prayer, and watch in the same with thanksgiving." Colossians 4:2 KJV

- "Praying **always** with all prayer and supplication in the Spirit, and watching thereunto with all perseverance and supplication for all saints." Ephesians 6:18 KJV

- "Be careful for nothing; but in **every thing** by prayer and supplication with thanksgiving let your requests be made known unto God." Philippians 4:6 KJV

These verses make it clear that we should pray all the time... in the good times and the bad times, on the mountains and in the valleys, in the car and kneeling by our bed, at home and at work, ...all the time.

No internet connection required...

Our Father is always there... always connected to our hearts.

BIBLE READING: 1 THESSALONIANS 5; PHILIPPIANS 4:4-8; ROMANS 12:12; COLOSSIANS 4:2; EPHESIANS 6:18

How Can I Be Strong?

"HAVE I NOT COMMANDED THEE? BE STRONG AND OF A GOOD COURAGE; BE NOT AFRAID, NEITHER BE THOU DISMAYED: FOR THE LORD THY GOD IS WITH THEE WHITHERSOEVER THOU GOEST." JOSHUA 1:9 KJV

I have an extreme phobia of public speaking, so throughout my entire life, I have gone above and beyond to avoid any circumstance that might require me to talk in front of a group of people. Even as a child in school, I was soft-spoken and shy, spending the day in a state of constant anxiety, hoping not to be called on by the teacher. For some reason, I have always been self-conscious about the sound of my voice.

Yet, in the past year or so, I have been invited to be a guest on several podcasts. As badly as I wanted to run in the other direction, I knew the way these opportunities came about was not coincidental. These opportunities were from God. The pull on my heart to share my writing testimony was a battle within myself because as afraid as I was to speak on camera, I knew God wanted me to. And if God had provided me an opportunity to share about Him and was giving me the message He wanted me to share, I had to face my fear and do it. If Jesus gave His life for me, how could I not use an opportunity that HE had placed right in front of me?

My fear of public speaking is a weakness, a weakness the enemy wants to use against me. However, in Joshua 1:9, God commands us to be strong and courageous. But how can I be strong and courageous when I am so afraid that my stomach twists in a knot, my heart pounds as if it should appear to be leaping from my chest, my voice quivers, and my mouth is so dry that I feel like I am going to choke? Well, the answer to that is in Joshua 1:9 too. We can be strong, courageous, and fearless because God is always with us.

BIBLE READING: JOSHUA 1:1-9

Free To Fly

"THEN SAID JESUS TO THOSE JEWS WHICH BELIEVED ON HIM, IF YE CONTINUE IN MY WORD, THEN ARE YE MY DISCIPLES INDEED; AND YE SHALL KNOW THE TRUTH, AND THE TRUTH SHALL MAKE YOU FREE." JOHN 8:31-32 KJV

When I was a kid, my dad decided to raise cattle for extra income. Now, note that my dad grew up in town, had never lived or worked on a farm, and knew nothing about farm animals, let alone cattle. Nevertheless, he rented sixteen acres of pasture land, put up a barbed wire fence, and went to the livestock market to purchase young beef cattle that he planned to fatten up and resell. He bought around thirty cows. Six of them were babies, and we soon learned they were too young to have been separated from their mother. My dad had to go to the local farm store and buy giant bottles and some sort of powdered formula for cows. In addition to the six babies that had to be bottle-fed, he had purchased one really old milk cow that looked like a bobblehead figurine from a distance because her head appeared abnormally large for her feeble body. His theory was, by purchasing this old grandma-looking cow, that the other cows would stick close to her because of her age. They did not. The other twenty-some-odd cows roamed the other side of the fence. Each day, when my parents got off from work and we checked on the cattle, it was not a question as to whether any of them had gotten out, but how far they had gone and where we had to go to find them. These cows were not satisfied with sixteen acres of oats. They wanted more... more than what that pasture had to offer.

In the same way, we often find ourselves searching... for fulfillment and purpose... for something on the other side of the fence that will finally make us feel complete and happy. In the depths of our hearts, we know we were meant for more. And friends, we are meant for more, but that more will not be found through anything in this world. In the Gospel of John, verses 8:31-32, Jesus says, "...if ye continue in my word, then are ye my disciples indeed; and ye shall know the truth, and the truth shall make you free" (KJV). As these verses detail, freedom comes in a relationship with Jesus... knowing Him and the truth in His Word... because through Him and only through Him do we have everlasting life.

This world is temporary. Jesus died to give us real freedom, but we have to accept it. We have to accept Jesus and believe in Him and His Word. Furthermore, if we truly believe, we will desire to grow and continue in His Word as His disciples.

And if we know the Truth, then we know only Jesus can satisfy that longing for fulfillment and purpose. Jesus says in John 4:14, "But whosoever drinketh of the water that I shall give him shall never thirst; but the water that I shall give him shall be in him a well of water springing up into everlasting life" (KJV).

BIBLE READING: JOHN 4:7-29; JOHN 8:12-32

I Cry... And He Hears

*"IN MY DISTRESS I CALLED UPON THE LORD,
AND CRIED UNTO MY GOD: HE HEARD MY
VOICE OUT OF HIS TEMPLE AND MY CRY
CAME BEFORE HIM, EVEN INTO HIS EARS."
PSALM 18:6 KJV*

It was pretty dark outside when I pulled up the drive. We had just moved into our new home, and because of the random things we had not yet put away, we were still parking our cars outside instead of in the garage. Let me share that I am not a night owl, so I was tired and ready to be home. But as I rounded the back of the car and stepped into the garage, something in my peripheral vision turned my head. I still have no idea how I saw it or why I would have even given it a second glance. In the slight glimmer of light coming from the security light on the side of the house, it appeared as nothing more than a tiny stick. But this tiny stick had a strange pattern, and I was no longer thinking about being tired. My senses were now on high alert, and my heart had dropped to my stomach. I knew my daughter would be arriving home in a couple of minutes, and as a mother, I could not help but panic that I would lose sight of this thing. Throughout my life, I've been told they are just as afraid of me as I am of them. Well, I have never bought that story, and I still do not. A snake is the one animal I fear, and add in some deadly venom, and my fear escalates into sheer horror. Trying to keep my eyes locked on my enemy, I stepped to the door and tried to yell for my husband in a hushed voice. I know that sounds contradictory, but for some reason, I felt that if my voice was too loud, it would alarm the snake. Yet, my husband was all the way on the other side of the house, and I was sure there was no way he would hear me. I have one of those voices that does not carry (even if I scream). But that night, he heard me, and as I pointed out the snake in the darkness, he was shocked I had seen this tiny copperhead's tail sticking out from beneath my car.

Have you ever been in an urgent situation where you yelled for someone and hoped they would hear you?

I love reading the Book of Psalms because of the depth of human emotion that resonates in the words. One of my favorite verses is Psalm 18:6, and I often repeat it out loud to remind myself that God hears my cries.

"In my distress I called upon the Lord, and cried unto my God: He heard my voice out of His temple, and my cry came before Him, even into His ears." Psalm 18:6 KJV

In Psalm 18, David acknowledges how God saved him from his enemies. He was afraid, and he called out to God. He knows God heard his cry and came to his rescue.

As Christians, we are not excluded from distress. In fact, sometimes I feel as if the devil is working overtime, filling my mind with worry. I have OCD, and the enemy seems to constantly prey on this area, using it to paralyze me and keep me from accomplishing anything meaningful. Just the other morning, as I sat on the floor before my time of prayer, out of nowhere, all these doubts and fears crept into my mind, and I began questioning my path in writing. In that moment, I felt so weighed down, pressed to the floor, as if a cloud of darkness was closing in around me. All I could do was cry out to God. I asked Him to please guide me... to clear the confusion... to lift my fears.

Later that morning, I had a conversation with my mom, and out of nowhere, she brought up a photo that I had given her for Christmas with a verse from a poem printed on it that I had written a while back.

"With every step, His hand squeezes mine,

and He whispers, "Take one more....

This is the only way to the mountain

that is better than the one before."

Friends, our enemy makes the trek through life as difficult as he can, but we must listen and cling to the words David wrote in Psalm 18. Our Father hears our cries. Trouble will come just as it did for David. And when it does, let us cry out to God just as David did. Let us take God's hand and let Him lead... for on the other side of the valley may be the highest mountaintop yet.

BIBLE READING: PSALM 18

Weeds

"But one thing is needful: and Mary hath chosen that good part, which shall not be taken away from her."
Luke 10:42 KJV

L et me begin by pointing out that I know nothing about plants. I do not have house plants, and the plants and flowers in our landscaping are there because I thought they would look good and not because of what I knew about them. Hence, many of my plants have a short life span. Honestly, I think the plants in the lawn and garden section of the store cower in fear as I walk past.

However, I have paid attention to my mother enough to know that weeds need to be removed because they take nutrients away from the desirable flowers and bushes. And the funny thing about weeds is that no special knowledge is required for them to grow. Weeds do not need to be pruned at a specific time of year or their bulbs separated, and they are not picky about full sun or shade. Weeds are absolutely maintenance-free if you want them to grow. That said, I am an expert. My garden has spectacular weeds.

The other day, I went out to weed our landscaping, and as I took in the bountiful array of weeds, I realized that I had procrastinated the chore way too long. I thought of Adam and Eve in the book of Genesis when they had disobeyed God. In Genesis 3:17-18, God says to Adam, "...Because thou has hearkened unto the voice of thy wife, and hast eaten of the tree, of which I commanded thee, saying, Thou shalt not eat of it: cursed is the ground for thy sake; in sorrow shalt thou eat of it all the days of thy life; Thorns also and thistles shall it bring forth to thee..." (KJV). Well, my flower beds had plenty of thorns and thistles.

As I plucked away at the multitude of invaders, I thought about how weeds are a result of Adam and Eve's disobedience. Even though weeds are a result of sin, I noticed that they are not all ugly. Some weeds like dandelions are actually beautiful. People spend time and a lot of money applying products to their lawns, trying to get rid of dandelions, but how many little girls pick dandelion bouquets or stick dandelions in their hair to look pretty?

As attractive weeds blended with my flowers, I had a hard time discerning the desirable from the undesirable, and if it is possible, I think the weeds actually multiplied as I was pulling them. I discovered that even the smallest weeds can have roots that seem to run as deep as those of a mighty white oak. As I finished, my attention was drawn to a bush at the far end of the house that had a mixture of small, shiny green leaves and larger, elongated, dull green leaves. Now, as I said, I am no expert, but I do not think a bush is supposed to have two entirely different types of leaves, so I pushed the branches apart to investigate. I am embarrassed to report that a weed had apparently started growing right at the base of the trunk and had camouflaged itself until it had become a full-fledged shrub. This thing was either going to have to be hewn down with a chainsaw, or since both the bush and the weed seemed to be flourishing, pretend they had created a symbiotic relationship and let it be. I voted for the latter.

Later on, I was still astonished at how far I had allowed the weeds to get out of control. And then I thought about how, at the end of the day, I often ask myself what I have accomplished. I am not talking about how many tasks I have completed but rather how I have used the day that the Lord has given me. Will anything that I did today make a difference tomorrow? Most of the time, I would have to honestly answer that question with a "no." I usually have worked non-stop all day at chores, like mopping and cleaning that, when I wake up in the morning, will appear as if I have never done them at all.

While most of us may not actually be battling thorns and thistles in a garden to provide food for our families, we do fight distractions that keep us from growing in our walk with God and hinder us from accomplishing God's purpose. In Luke 10, Jesus visits the home of two sisters, Mary and Martha. Mary sits with Jesus, absorbing what He has to say, while Martha works on the meal. Martha becomes upset that Mary is not helping, but Jesus says to her, "...Martha, Martha, thou art careful and troubled about many things: But one thing is needful: and Mary hath chosen that good part, which shall not be taken away from her" (Luke 10:41-42 KJV).

I find that all of these daily chores and distractions of the world are like weeds. The weeds start small but before long, they have taken up so much time that they have absorbed all of the nutrition out of the most important thing, a relationship with our Heavenly Father. Each day is a gift from God. It is important to prioritize that one thing Jesus says is needed. Time with our Savior brings us closer to Him and nurtures our relationship with Him. While daily chores are needed and work is a requirement, is it the work God is calling us to do or are we allowing our work to become a ritual and allowing meaningless tasks to become weeds, absorbing the time we should be giving to God. After all, God has a plan for our lives, and it is in the time we spend with Him that we discover that plan.

I do not want to wake up tomorrow realizing that there is not a shred of evidence of what I did yesterday. I want to wake up to a better tomorrow because of what I do today.

BIBLE READING: LUKE 10; GENESIS 3:17-18

Through the Eyes of a Child

"VERILY I SAY UNTO YOU, WHOSOEVER SHALL NOT RECEIVE THE KINGDOM OF GOD AS A LITTLE CHILD, HE SHALL NOT ENTER THEREIN." MARK 10:15 KJV

A little girl with a lot to say chatters from the passenger seat. "You know what, Mommy?"

"What?" I reply with curiosity.

"I sure am glad Eve ate that apple."

I remain speechless for a moment as I try to wrap my mind around my daughter's statement. I think of Eve disobeying

God by eating the fruit He had told her not to eat. *Eve could eat from any tree in the garden except for the tree of the knowledge of good and evil, but she gives in to temptation. Eve eats the fruit of the only tree she was not to partake of and then gives the fruit to Adam. This disobedience brings sin into the world, and that sin brings death. Man would no longer live the easy life in paradise but would have to work for provisions. Not only does man have to labor for food, but he will have obstacles to overcome. Genesis 3:17 says, "...cursed is the ground for thy sake..." (KJV). Mankind now has to battle weeds as he labors for food. On top of this, women will have to endure physical pain in childbirth.*

So, where is the upside to Eve's choice to follow the serpent's advice? I cannot wait to hear her reasoning, so I ask, "Oh. Why is that?"

"Well, if Eve didn't eat that apple, snakes would have legs. And it would be really creepy to see a snake running through the yard."

A child's perception sometimes stumps adults. Maturity brings responsibility, and with that responsibility comes obstacles and worry. Pessimism trumps optimism as life brings storm after storm, and those storms cause tree after tree to fall across the road, blocking the way. However, adults can learn so much from children. As imaginative as her conclusion was, my daughter uncovered her own positive from Eve's disobedience. Now I am not saying that Eve's choice to disobey God was in any way good, but my daughter had found her own speck of light in the darkness. Eve's bad decision allowed my daughter to play outside without the worry of encountering a snake speeding through the yard on legs.

"And we know that all things work together for good to them that love God, to them who are the called according to his purpose" (Romans 8:28 KJV).

When those trees block the path, God will provide a detour for those who trust him. As Christians in a dark world, we need to shine light and reflect the hope a relationship with Jesus gives us. Sometimes we need to look at things through the eyes of a child. Children do not stress out about their needs being taken care of. They trust that their parents will take care of them. In the same way, Christians should put their trust in their Heavenly Father. In Mark 10:15, Jesus says, "Verily I say unto you, Whosoever shall not receive the kingdom of God as a little child, he shall not enter therein" (KJV). Of course, God does not promise a smooth travel, but He promises to be there to guide the journey. Just as a little girl discovered a slice of chocolate cake in the middle of the salad bar, those who have accepted Christ as their savior can find light in the darkest times because they have the assurance of having their own personal tour guide until they reach their eternal Heavenly destination. And, if a person does not have that assurance, it is only a prayer away.

BIBLE READING: MARK 10:13-27; GENESIS 3; ROMANS 8:28

Coordinates (X, Why?)

"... AND WHO KNOWETH WHETHER THOU ART COME TO THE KINGDOM FOR SUCH A TIME AS THIS?" ESTHER 4:14 KJV

One evening back in 1995, I stopped at a Krystal fast-food restaurant to get my grandmother some of those little burgers she loved so much. As I pulled away from the drive-thru window, a handsome guy in another car motioned for me to roll down my window. We introduced ourselves and then went our own way. Several months later, I began working for a credit union at a local furniture manufacturing company. Well, guess who was also employed there and came in to cash his paycheck? Yep. It was that handsome guy who I had met at Krystal's a few months earlier.

Jumping ahead to the present, I have been married to that handsome guy for almost twenty-six years, and we have two grown children. So, was it merely a coincidence that we crossed paths in the parking lot of Krystal's all those years ago and then just happened to end up working at the same place in the next town over from where we lived? Absolutely not. It was God's providence that put us both in that parking lot at Krystal's that day. It was God's providence that made our paths cross again with our jobs. It was God's providence because twenty-nine years later, I am more in love with that handsome guy than ever, and we are blessed with an amazing family.

As we go through life, we never know why we might end up in a certain place or meet a particular person. Look at some examples in the Bible.

- Was it a coincidence that Joseph's father sent him to check on his brothers on that particular day? Was it a coincidence that those merchants just happened to pass by, purchase Joseph, and sell him to Potiphar? As we know, those events later put Joseph in a position to save his brothers.

- What about Esther? She was an orphaned Jewish girl who was raised by her uncle. She became queen and, because of her position, she was able to save the Jewish people. As Esther 4:14 explains, Esther's position as queen was no coincidence. "...and who knoweth whether thou art come to the kingdom for such a time as this?" (Esther 4:14 KJV).

- Nehemiah was a cupbearer to the king. In Nehemiah 1:11, as Nehemiah prays for God to use him to rebuild the walls of Jerusalem, he recognizes that this position is not a coincidence. "O Lord, I beseech thee, let now thine ear be attentive to the prayer of thy servant, and to the prayer of thy servants, who desire to fear thy name: and prosper, I pray thee, thy servant this day, and grant him mercy in the sight of this man. For I was the king's cupbearer." (Nehemiah 1:11 KJV). Nehemiah says, "...for I was the king's cupbearer...," meaning his position gave him the ability to ask the king for help.

God has a plan even if we don't see it right away. I believe, that if we are Christians, God has each of us exactly where He needs us to be. Sometimes, we all question where we are in life. But God knows. After all, Jeremiah 29:11 (KJV) says, "For I know the thoughts that I think toward you, saith the Lord, thoughts of peace, and not of evil, to give you an expected end."

The important thing is that we glorify God wherever we are, and He will take care of the rest.

"And whatsoever ye do, do it heartily, as to the Lord, and not unto men." Colossians 3:23 KJV.

BIBLE READING: ESTHER 4; NEHEMIAH 1:11; JEREMIAH 29:11; COLOSSIANS 3:23

Need Directions?

"TRUST IN THE LORD WITH ALL THINE HEART; AND LEAN NOT UNTO THINE OWN UNDERSTANDING. IN ALL THY WAYS ACKNOWLEDGE HIM, AND HE SHALL DIRECT THY PATHS." PROVERBS 3:5-6 KJV

When I woke up this morning, I had a list formed in my mind of everything that I was going to get done before going with my daughter to the dentist. However, the first thing on the list took longer than I anticipated, and I was discouraged when it was time to leave because I had not achieved my goal. Nonetheless, whether my goal was achieved or not, it was time to go.

My daughter has her driver's license, so in order for her to miss less time from school, she drove separately so she could go straight to class without having to go all the way back home. I pulled out of the driveway first, and she should have been close behind me. It is important to note that she had just been to the dentist the previous week. This was a follow-up appointment.

When I arrived at the dentist, I waited in the car for her before going in. And I waited. And I waited some more. Honestly, I started to get concerned. Just as I picked up my phone to check her location, she pulled into the parking lot. When I asked her what had taken her so long, her response was, "I went to the wrong dentist." Of course, I couldn't help but point out that we had just been there five days ago and found humor in her actually going to the wrong dentist's office (especially when we have been going to this office for several years). But, in all fairness, I had driven her the last time, and she admitted she hadn't been paying attention. I know when I am not in the driver's seat, I am usually taking in the scenery, not the route...(like mother, like daughter, I suppose.)

As I waited in the lobby for my daughter to see the dentist, I thought about her little detour. She thought she knew the way, so she didn't ask for help or use her GPS.

Then, I thought about my morning and how I woke up with my steps for the day already planned. Of course, having goals and a list of things to accomplish is part of life, and we are supposed to work. However, just because I think I know how my day should go and what I need to accomplish, that may not be what God wants me to accomplish.

So, as I sat staring into space in the dentist's office, I asked myself how many times that I consult God, asking for directions. Sure, I go to him every morning. But do I truly, with an open heart ask, "God what do you want me to do today?," and then keep my eyes and ears open and focused on the opportunities that He may present me with throughout the day? Do I listen to the voice that tells me to stop going in my direction and send a text to the person God suddenly laid on my heart? Do I take the time to notice that God has put someone right in front of me that needs to hear about Jesus?

I need God's direction in every part of my life and every part of my day. After all, my GPS brings me back to the same list every morning. God may have a different route planned for my day.

BIBLE READING: PROVERBS 3

Warrior Sisters

"TWO ARE BETTER THAN ONE; BECAUSE THEY HAVE A GOOD REWARD FOR THEIR LABOUR." ECCLESIASTES 4:9 KJV

I work out every morning, and even though I have done so for years, I still have to focus when I do abdominal exercises. Since I delivered both of my children via c-section, it has taken time to strengthen the muscle tissue in my stomach. So, when I do sit-ups or crunches, if I do not consciously force myself to use my abdominal muscles, my back will come to the rescue as if to say, "Don't worry, stomach muscles. I'm here. Together, we got this."

When one part of our body is weaker or not functioning properly, sometimes other stronger parts kick in to pick up the slack. In 1 Corinthians 12, Paul refers to believers as members of the body of Christ. We have different talents and roles to play in serving God and fulfilling His purpose. But just as my back muscles jump in to help out my stomach muscles, or my hand reaches down to offer relief to an itch on my leg, as Christians, we need to be attentive to the bonds we have as the body of Christ because we have much to offer each other. This goes beyond fellowship and greeting each other on Sunday morning. I am talking about how each part of the body works together to support the other. Our heart pumps blood carrying oxygen through our body, but without our lungs to take in the oxygen, what is that blood going to deliver?

In Romans 1:12, Paul longs to see the Romans not just for how he could help them, but how they could comfort and encourage each other. He says, "That is, that I may be comforted together with you by the mutual faith both of you and me" (Romans 1:12 KJV).

When I read this verse, I cannot help but think of my 'Warrior Sister.' We call ourselves 'Warrior Sisters' because each morning we text each other words of encouragement, with a reminder to put on our spiritual armor and keep our shields up. For example, one recent text from my 'Warrior Sister' simply said, *Shields UP! God goes before us... And behind us... AND beside us.*

Why do we do this every day? Because the enemy is always lurking, ready to attack. Satan is hovering in the shadows, seeking to offer every distraction and throw as many hurdles in front of us as he can so that we lose focus and will not keep our attention on what God has for us to accomplish.

Ecclesiastes 4:9-10 says, "Two are better than one; because they have a good reward for their labour. For if they fall, the one will lift up his fellow: but woe to him that is alone when he falleth; for he hath not another to help him up" (KJV). When we put on our armor, we each have our shield of faith. But when we stand together we can form a wall with those shields just like the Roman soldiers.

This is the connection that I have with my "Warrior Sister." It is the connection that says, "Don't worry. Together we got this."

I pray we will remember that as children of God, we are one body, the body of Christ. And, as the body of Christ, we should be comforting and encouraging each other in our faith with that unified connection that says, "Don't worry. Together we got this."

BIBLE READING: ROMANS 1:12; ECCLESIASTES 4:9-10; 1 CORINTHIANS 12

Adjusting the Thermostat

"I KNOW THY WORKS, THAT THOU ART NEITHER COLD NOR HOT: I WOULD THOU WERT COLD OR HOT. SO THEN BECAUSE THOU ART LUKEWARM, AND NEITHER COLD NOR HOT, I WILL SPUE THEE OUT OF MY MOUTH." REVELATION 3:15-16 KJV

I am a cold-natured person with absolutely no tolerance for frigid temperatures, so if I know I am going to be somewhere I could get cold, I wear layers and pack blankets, gloves, a hat, and anything else I can think of that might eliminate the agony. On the other hand, my children cannot stand to be hot, so the summer months seem to be an endless battle when it comes to the thermostat setting.

But have you ever noticed that if the temperature is at a comfortable level for our body, we think nothing of it?

In Revelation 3:14-21, Jesus finishes His messages to the churches by addressing the church in Laodicea. To say the least, Jesus is not pleased with this church. In fact, in so many words, He says this church makes Him sick. "I know thy works, that thou art neither cold nor hot: I would thou wert cold or hot. So then because thou art lukewarm, and neither cold nor hot, I will spue thee out of my mouth" (Revelation 3:15-16 KJV).

He would prefer them to either have true faith and follow Him diligently or not proclaim to be His followers at all. But it sickens Him that they are saying they are rich in faith when they are not. The problem is that they are oblivious to their spiritual temperature. Jesus says, "Because thou sayest, I am rich, and increased with goods, and have need of nothing; and knowest not that thou art wretched, and miserable, and poor, and blind, and naked" (Revelation 3:17 KJV).

As I illustrated in my example at the beginning of this post, if one is hot or cold, that person is aware of it. In the same way, if one is truly a follower of Christ, one will desire to study the Bible and live by God's Word. That person will want to spend time with the Savior and grow closer to Him. That person will produce spiritual fruit and be passionate about sharing the Gospel and the love of Jesus. However, if one is not a believer in Christ, that person is fully aware that Jesus is not in his or her life.

The church members in Laodicea are unaware of their spiritual temperature because, as Jesus said in verse 16, they are "lukewarm." They are in this so-called comfort zone, convinced they are right with God while living their lives as they please.

So, why are Jesus's words to them so harsh and reprimanding? Why is he sending them this warning? The answer is in Revelation 3:19 where Jesus explains, "As many as I love, I rebuke and chasten: be zealous therefore, and repent" (KJV). Jesus reprimands those that he loves. He does not want anyone to be separated from Him. In fact, the very next verse details the close and personal relationship that He desires with each and every person. He says, "Behold, I stand at the door, and knock: if any man hear my voice, and open the door, I will come in to him, and will sup with him, and he with me" (Revelation 3:20 KJV). To share a meal with someone means to have a one-on-one interaction and conversation. He wants to come into our lives, and He wants us to know Him personally. But we have to let Him in. And if we sincerely ask Him in, we should no longer desire to live according to the ways of the world.

As we reflect on our spiritual temperature, I pray that our reading is high because Jesus said, "He that is not with me is against me..." (Matthew 12:30 KJV).

BIBLE READING: REVELATION 3:14-21; MATTHEW 12:30

Paid In Full

"FOR GOD SO LOVED THE WORLD, THAT HE GAVE HIS ONLY BEGOTTEN SON, THAT WHOSOEVER BELIEVETH IN HIM SHOULD NOT PERISH, BUT HAVE EVERLASTING LIFE."
JOHN 3:16 KJV

She stands in line, the thick stack of papers crinkling between her trembling fingers. Squeezing her eyes closed, she swallows the baseball-size lump in her throat. *How could I have committed so many violations? What am I going to do? I can't pay for all these tickets.* Just as the thought passes through her mind, another scream echoes from the front of the line and then fades into the distance. She has heard a lot of screams today. *Probably, because like me, they can't afford to pay the court,* she thinks to herself.

As the line moves forward, she tries her best to block out her surroundings, and before she realizes it, only one person is left in front of her. Water pools in her eyes and trickles down her face as the man in front of her approaches the bench. She drops her head hoping no one will notice her tears.

Startling her, a piercing wail causes her to jerk her head up. The man in front of her is gone, but his painful shrieks still reverberate around her.

"Next," a voice booms from the bench.

She takes a step toward the bench wondering where the voice came from. No one appears to be behind the desk, so she takes another step, thinking maybe someone will pop up.

"Next!" the voice thunders louder.

Her stomach twists, and the papers fly from her hands. In a panic, she falls to the floor snatching them up as fast as she can. Suddenly, another set of hands is picking up the papers too.

"Ma'am, it looks like you are going to owe a pretty hefty fine."

She lifts her eyes to meet the face attached to the helping hands. "Y-yes. It seems that I have made more than a few bad choices." She pulls in a shallow breath and takes the stack of papers from the man's extended hand. "Mistakes that I can't pay for."

The man tucks his hand under her elbow and tugs her to her feet. "How about I just pay this debt for you?"

"What?" Her pitch rises in surprise.

"I asked if I could pay the debt for you," he says without skipping a beat.

"Oh, if you could, I would pay you back. I promise." Relief floods through her words.

"No need, ma'am. Just accept this payment as my gift to you."

"I-I d-don't know what to say. I can't believe you would do this for me. Thank you... thank you so much," she sputters out as the sounds of all those piercing screams replay in her mind.

He takes the stack of papers from her hands and steps up to the desk. Then, he pulls a rusty nail from his pocket and dips it in a bottle of red ink on the table. Red droplets drip onto the pages as he scribbles the words "PAID IN FULL" on each one.

After he is finished, he turns, lifts his hand, and wipes his fingertips beneath her eyes, swiping away the tears. "It is taken care of. You are free."

"Th-thank you." She pivots to walk away but turns back. "Sir, why would you do this for me? I know lots of people here today haven't been able to pay. Why me?"

"Ma'am, I've already paid the debt for everyone here. It's just that some wouldn't accept my gift."

The bloodcurdling cries echo through her head once more, and she crinkles her forehead in confusion. "But why... why would anyone not accept your gift?"

In the above fictional story, the character questions why anyone would refuse such a gift. Yet, in reality, the gift of a debt paid in full by a Savior who loved us so much that HE suffered and shed His own blood in our place is rejected by many.

"For all have sinned, and come short of the glory of God." Romans 3:23 KJV

But...

"For God so loved the world, that He gave His only begotten Son, that whosoever believeth in Him should not perish, but have everlasting life." John 3:16 KJV

Every person past and present except for Jesus has sinned. Jesus went to that cross as an innocent lamb and gave His life shedding His own blood to pay the debt for our sins. But we have to accept the payment He made for us. We have to believe that He died and rose again. If we have accepted His gift and asked Him to be our Lord and Savior, the debt we owe for all the mistakes we have made... all of those bad choices... all those sins have been stamped "PAID IN FULL" with the blood of Jesus. Those chains that would have bound us into forever darkness and eternal punishment have been broken, and we are free.

BIBLE READING: JOHN 3:16; ROMANS 3:23

Always A Purpose for the Season

"TO EVERY THING THERE IS A SEASON, AND A TIME TO EVERY PURPOSE UNDER THE HEAVEN." ECCLESIASTES 3:1 KJV

How many times I have read this verse, yet it was not until recently that the depth of these words penetrated to the core of my soul.

Earlier this year, my family had to say goodbye to our pet of thirteen and a half years. But to us, she was not just a pet, she was a member of our family. My son was seven, and my daughter was four when we got our beautiful, brindle boxer. I knew my kids would love her, but honestly, I never imagined they would have spent so much time and have such a true and unbreakable bond with her. From the time Lucy joined our family at six weeks old, she was their best friend. They played games with her, read to her, had tea parties with her, and dressed her in all sorts of costumes. I would have thought most dogs might have gotten frustrated or even hid, but Lucy enjoyed every minute. The three of them grew up together.

And now, my son and my daughter are off to college, embarking on their own new journeys, while my husband and I are adjusting to an empty nest.

"To every thing there is a season..." (Ecclesiastes 3:1 KJV).

Lucy was there every step of the way as my kids grew, and as hard it was to say goodbye (oh... how I miss her so bad and cry now still as I write this), we were so blessed to have been able to share so many years with her. Lucy lived beyond the age of most in her breed, and in my heart, I know she held on so long for my children. They were her purpose. A new season is beginning for my children as they continue to find the path God has created for them, and a new season is beginning for my husband and me as we learn to let go and let them find their path.

But friends, let us not take one day in these seasons for granted because each day has its purpose.

"...and a time to every purpose under the heaven." Ecclesiastes 3:1 KJV

Let us wake up each morning with our focus on His purpose for the coming day of the present season of our lives. Let us embrace every moment.

BIBLE READING: ECCLESIASTES 3

A Reflection of Truth

"So God created man in His own image, in the image of God created He him; male and female created He them." Genesis 1:27 KJV

I have to admit that I have often struggled with self-image, especially when I was younger. I have always been petite, hovering around a hundred pounds. And, while I have never had a weight problem, magazine photos, television, and comments that I would hear as a child led me to believe an attractive woman had a specific figure, one with curves in the right places. I remember when I was around thirteen or fourteen years old, my paternal grandmother turned me sideways in the mirror and commented that I was getting the battle of the bulge because my stomach pooched out a little. Now, when my grandmother pointed this out, she did not mean any harm. She made the same comments regarding herself and was always concerned with having a perfect complexion. I think this must have been instilled in her earlier in life. But from then on, when I looked in the mirror, I saw a stick with spindly legs, and the only curve was the stomach that I couldn't flatten no matter how hard I sucked in. When I looked in the mirror, I did not see the truth.

The Bible states, "So God created man in His own image, in the image of God created He him; male and female created He them" (Genesis 1:27 KJV). We are created in the image of God.

As we read on, chapter two describes God forming Adam and Eve. We are told how God made Adam from the dust of the ground and breathed air into him (Genesis 2:7). We are told how God took one of Adam's ribs and created Eve (Genesis 2:21-22).

What are we not told? We are not told of Adam's stature, his hair color, or if he had broad shoulders. We are not told if Eve had washboard abs, a thin waistline, or a flawless complexion.

And, not only is it important to note that we are created in the image of God, but also that we are created by the hand of God.

Psalm 139:13-14 details, "For thou hast possessed my reins: thou hast covered me in my mother's womb. I will praise thee; for I am fearfully and wonderfully made: marvelous are thy works..." (KJV). And in Ephesians 2:10, Paul writes, "For we are workmanship, created in Christ Jesus unto good works..." (KJV). When we look in the mirror, we are looking at a person modeled after God's own image and molded by His very hands. How can we see any flaw in a piece of art created by God? How can we not look in the mirror and see a masterpiece?

So, today, when you look in the mirror, remember you are a specially, hand-crafted, one-of-a-kind created by God in the image of God.

BIBLE READING: GENESIS 1:27; GENESIS 2; PSALM 139:13-14; EPH-ESIANS 2:10

The Good Fruit

*"SET YOUR AFFECTION ON THINGS ABOVE,
NOT ON THINGS ON THE EARTH."
COLOSSIANS 3:2 KJV*

One of our previous homes had a line of apple trees paralleling one edge of our property. Our dog was only a few years old then and still full of energy. We used to find it amusing that she loved the apples but would never eat the ones on the ground. Instead, she would take a running leap and snatch the fresh ones from the trees.

In Galatians 5:19-21, Paul details a list of works or bad fruit that we should not be producing or involved with as followers of Christ. He even specifies that these things will keep us from Heaven.

"Now the works of the flesh are manifest, which are these; Adultery, fornication, uncleanness, lasciviousness, idolatry, witchcraft, hatred, variance, emulations, wrath, strife, seditions, heresies, envyings, murders, drunkenness, revellings, and such like: of the which I tell you before, as I have also told you in time past, that they which do such things shall not inherit the kingdom of God." Galatians 5:19-21 KJV

But Paul does not leave us hanging with just a list of things not to do. He goes on to list the traits that a follower of Christ should aspire to possess.

"But the fruit of the Spirit is love, joy, peace, longsuffering, gentleness, goodness, faith, meekness, temperance: against such there is no law." Galatians 5:22-23 KJV

As I read these verses, the memory of our dog picking fresh apples popped into my mind. She did not want the apples on the ground that could have possibly begun to rot or that might have worms or bees in them. She wanted the good apples on the tree way above her head, even if that meant putting in a lot more effort to get them.

The things Paul notes that will keep one from the kingdom of God are of the flesh or worldly desires that the devil loves to use as temptations in order to lure followers away from Christ. But the good fruit that Paul shares are qualities that we should produce more and more of as we grow closer in our walk with

Christ. Just as our dog recognized the dangers in the rotten fruit on the ground and yearned for the good fruit above her, we should not focus on worldly desires but on things above and becoming more like Jesus in all we say and do.

Bible Reading: Galatians 5; Colossians 3:2

Only By His Power

"AND WHAT IS THE EXCEEDING GREATNESS
OF HIS POWER TO US-WARD WHO BELIEVE,
ACCORDING TO THE WORKING OF HIS
MIGHTY POWER, WHICH HE WROUGHT
IN CHRIST, WHEN HE RAISED HIM FROM
THE DEAD, AND SET HIM AT HIS OWN
RIGHT HAND IN THE HEAVENLY PLACES."
EPHESIANS 1:19-20 KJV

A few months ago, I ordered an over-the-toilet cabinet. I chose this particular one because it matched the vanity cabinet in our guest bathroom, and since it was in the same product line as the vanity that I was pleased with, I failed to read the reviews. When the cabinet came, I spread a rug out in the garage and assembled the cabinet, and I have to say, it looked good. I could not wait to see it in the bathroom. After a bit of maneuvering, I finally got it inside only to discover it was too short to fit over the toilet. Discouraged, thinking I must have done something wrong in the assembly, I went to the website and found that I was not the only person to have had this problem. I believe one person even commented in a review that the product must not have been tested with a real toilet.

I had been so excited to find a cabinet that perfectly matched the vanity that I failed to check the measurements printed on the box. I assumed since it was made to go over the toilet, and we had a standard-size commode, it was sure to fit. I immediately called the store only to be told that if I disassembled it, I could return it. However, one of the store clerks admitted, after looking at the measurements on the box, that this shelf would not fit over any toilet they sold.

In short, I did not return the cabinet. I was not disassembling it, and I still liked it because it matched. Instead, the project turned into adapting and overcoming. I removed the cabinet from the stand, which should have fit over the toilet. My husband adapted the back of the cabinet with supports so it could be mounted to the wall.

My point is this cabinet was designed with all of these pieces. The directions were clear and precise. Yet, with all of the engineering and perfectly cut boards, in the end, the product could not do what it was designed to do.

But, when I think of our bodies and the cells, organs, and systems that all perform at the same time, the complexity of our brains and the amount of information that we can store and recall, and add to that, the different methods in which we each process that information and create, it is unfathomable that we could be here by any other means than the all-powerful God who created us in His image. I know that our God created and engineered each and every one of us. He gave some of us a knack for math and numbers, while others He instilled an imagination to create and design. The list of each of our special gifts can go on and on.

That brings me to Ephesians 1:19-20, which states, "And what is the exceeding greatness of His power to us-ward who believe, according to the working of His mighty power, Which He wrought in Christ, when He raised Him from the dead, and set Him at His own right hand in the Heavenly places" (KJV). God, who created the Heavens and the earth, the sun and the moon, the oceans and fish, the birds and the trees, and every living thing is the God who loves us so much that He sent His Son to die for each of us. By His great power, He raised Jesus from the dead. And our all-powerful God wants a personal relationship with each of us. Anytime, anywhere, we can pray and talk to the God who spoke everything into existence.

BIBLE READING: EPHESIANS 1:19-20; GENESIS 1-2

Heart Transplant

"A NEW HEART ALSO WILL I GIVE YOU, AND A NEW SPIRIT WILL I PUT WITHIN YOU: AND I WILL TAKE AWAY THE STONY HEART OUT OF YOUR FLESH, AND I WILL GIVE YOU AN HEART OF FLESH." EZEKIEL 36:26 KJV

Lying on the hospital bed, he stares up at the fluorescent light. Spots fill his vision as his unblinking eyes get lost in the glare. He falls into some sort of trance as if he is floating in space, looking at himself from the outside. His thoughts walk him through the journey that brought him here. He has had money. He has had fame. He has had success. The world has treated him well. High after high, he has kept climbing the limbs the world had to offer in search of the ultimate high. But he hadn't found true happiness yet. He had never felt that real inner joy he was in search of. So, he knew he hadn't climbed high enough. But now, even though he is still considered a young man, it seems the climb may be over. The doctors have told him he has a condition. The muscle in his heart is slowly hardening, and soon, it will not be able to pump blood through his body anymore. His death will be a long and painful one.

The door to the room creaks open and slams with a thud. In a moment, his doctor is standing over him, and the young man blinks to clear the spots and bring the doctor into focus.

"Son, I have some news for you," the doctor says in a humble voice. "We have the heart for your transplant."

The young man narrows his eyes as he gazes up at the doctor. "But I thought there was only one person who could give me a replacement."

"Yes." The doctor sits on the edge of the bed. "Your father said he would give anything so you could live. He has already made the sacrifice. All we need to do now is perform the surgery, and then you will be like new. Of course, you will have to make some changes to your lifestyle. Your body will need to accept this new heart, and I'm sure you want to take care of this one. You don't want to waste this second chance."

"No, I don't want it, but thanks anyway."

The doctor tilts his head and glares at the young man in disbelief. "What do you mean you don't want it? Your father already sacrificed his life to give you his heart. The process was brutal, and he suffered in agonizing pain. Your father died to give you life. And you are telling me that you don't want his heart?"

The young man's jawline hardens, and he speaks in a flat voice. "No. I don't."

"I don't understand. Why would you waste your father's sacrifice?" The doctor shakes his head in confusion.

"Because if I take that heart, I will have to change. I will have to stop doing the things that make me somebody in this world." The young man squeezes his eyes closed. "But mostly because if I accept that heart, I am acknowledging that my father loved me that much. He loved me enough to die for me."

In Luke 19, as Jesus approaches Jerusalem, the crowd is rejoicing and praising God. The scene is depicted in Luke 19:37-38 as it says, "And when he was come nigh, even now at the descent of the mount of Olives, the whole multitude of the disciples began to rejoice and praise God with a loud voice for all the mighty works that they had seen; Saying Blessed be the

King that cometh in the name of the Lord: peace in heaven, and glory in the highest" (KJV). Then, a few verses later, Jesus looks out over the city and weeps. Luke 19:41 states, "And when he was come near, he beheld the city, and wept over it" (KJV).

Of course, we know the story. It's not long before the people are yelling, "...Crucify Him, crucify Him" (Luke 23:21 KJV).

Could you imagine standing in a crowd before Jesus and yelling "Crucify him"? Although my opening is fictional, the premise holds truth. We have the word of God. We know the prophecy foretold hundreds and hundreds of years before Jesus came. Isaiah 53:5 details, "But he was wounded for our transgressions, he was bruised for our iniquities: the chastisement of our peace was upon Him; and with his stripes we are healed" (KJV). Yet, some still refuse to accept His gift of salvation.

Today, as I sit here and ponder on our Savior and the suffering he endured, His hands and feet nailed to the cross, and His body hanging there, bearing all of that pain and torture in my place, I know I never want to take that kind of love for granted. And then I think of how Jesus cried as He looked at Jerusalem, and I can only imagine the tears He must shed now when His sacrifice is ignored or rejected.

He already paid the price for you and for me. He already hung on that cross for you and for me.

Ezekiel 36:26 says, "A new heart also will I give you, and a new spirit will I put within you: and I will take away the stony heart our of your flesh, and I will give you an heart of flesh" (KJV). A new heart is waiting... but we have to accept it.

BibleReading: Ezekiel 36:26; Isaiah 53:5; Luke 19:37-41; Luke 23:21-46

Eyes on Jesus

"WHEREFORE SEEING WE ALSO ARE COMPASSED ABOUT WITH SO GREAT A

CLOUD OF WITNESSES, LET US LAY ASIDE EVERY WEIGHT, AND THE SIN WHICH DOTH SO EASILY BESET US, AND LET US RUN WITH PATIENCE THE RACE THAT IS SET BEFORE

US, LOOKING UNTO JESUS THE AUTHOR AND FINISHER OF OUR FAITH..." HEBREWS 12:1-2 KJV

P rior to this week, I did not see how our schedule could get any busier, but it did. And maybe it was not that there was more to do, but that I allowed it to consume and overwhelm me. It was as if my list of chores was swirling around me in a cyclone. And then, as I began to jump from task to task without finishing one before moving to another, I was no longer in the middle of the tornado, getting dizzy from watching it rotate. Instead, my frustration had me spinning with it.

So, I had to stop myself and take a moment to reassess and reprioritize. Upon doing so, for some reason, I recalled a fishing trip my family had taken several years back. My husband loves to fish, and my children and I had never been fishing in the ocean, so we thought it would be a fun weekend getaway. I scheduled a charter boat for the four of us, and since it was our first time, I only opted for the half-day trip.

My son could not have had his fishing pole in the water longer than two minutes before he became seasick and passed it off to me. A couple of minutes later, my daughter did the same. Now, at this point, I have three fishing poles, and my stomach is starting to churn. We were quite a way out in the ocean, but yet, in the distance, I could still see the shore. And, on the shore, I could see the top of a tower rising above everything else, so I locked my eyes on the tower. Keeping my focus on a fixed object seemed to ease my queasiness.

I realized that this recollection actually had a valuable lesson. Just as I had kept my focus on the tower to keep the rocking waves from making me ill, keeping our eyes focused on Jesus will keep the monotony of our daily lives and the stresses of living in this world from bringing us down.

"...let us run with patience the race that is set before us, Looking unto Jesus the author and finisher of our faith..." Hebrews 12:1-2 KJV.

Sometimes, I have to remind myself that the race I am running is not about my list of chores. The race I am running is for my Savior. In order to cross that finish line, I have to keep my eyes on Him, remembering that I am not in this race for my purpose but to fulfill His purpose for me.

In 1 Corinthians, chapter 9, Paul details how the race should be run. I pray that we can run our race as Paul did.

"I therefore so run, not as uncertainly; so fight I, not as one that beateth the air: But I keep under my body, and bring it into subjection: lest that by any means, when I have preached to others, I myself should be a castaway" (1 Corinthians 9:26-27 KJV).

BIBLE READING: HEBREWS 12; 1 CORINTHIANS 9:26-27

Letting Go

"WHICH OF YOU BY TAKING THOUGHT CAN ADD ONE CUBIT UNTO HIS STATURE?"
MATTHEW 6:27 KJV

I am a worrier who desires order and a clear-cut plan without surprises (unless I am penning a novel). That said, I have what I sometimes refer to as "my bubble." In my bubble, everything is under control. In my bubble, floors are clean, and stainless appliances are free of fingerprints. In my bubble, all projects are completed way before a deadline. In my bubble, drama does not exist. My bubble is a worry-free zone.

However, I cannot stay in my bubble because life is happening in the real world. And... in the real world... outside my bubble, people leave fingerprints on the stainless refrigerator right after I polish it. Outside my bubble, my kids wait until 11:50 p.m. to complete a seven-page paper that is due at midnight. Outside my bubble, my children are old enough to get behind the wheel of a car and make their own choices, and I can no longer protect them every minute. Outside my bubble, anything could go wrong. Outside my bubble, the devil whispers all those "what ifs" and creates chaos. So, of course, I pray. I ask God to take the worries because 1 Peter 5:7 says, "Casting all your care upon him; for He careth for you" (KJV). So, what's the problem?

Let me share another example. When my husband and I were building our house (I suppose I should clarify that my husband was building our house, and I attempted to help), he constructed the exterior walls in sixteen-foot sections. Then, as we would stand the sections up one by one, he would nail them in place. Now would be a good time to note that I am horrified of heights, and the back side of the house is extremely high. Before the walls were in place, I would not get within five feet of the edge. If I did, I would feel my equilibrium shift, and my heartbeat would take off in a sprint. So, along the back of the house, every wall we put in place brought worry. If I did not maintain control of that wall and pushed it too far, it could fall over the edge. If the wall went over the edge, I could forget to let go which would take me over the edge. *One worry always seems to lead to another.* Of course, my husband was holding the wall too, so my worries were not rational but rather a result of my fear. And, because of that fear, I would only push each section seven-eighths of the way up, causing my husband to have to lift the wall and me the rest of the way until the wall was straight up and down. You see, I thought that if I kept the wall slightly shifted back toward me, I could keep it under control, and it would not go crashing over the side.

I often find myself using this same concept with worries that I take to God in prayer. I pray and ask God to carry a burden, but I do not completely let go. Just like I kept the wall slightly tilted back, I take the problem to God, but then I keep trying to fix it myself, which usually leads to disaster and the creation of something new to worry about.

As I read 1 Peter 5:7, one specific word stands out. The verse uses the word "cast" to instruct us what to do with worries. In other words, we are to throw our worries on Him, and throwing requires letting go. The verse does not say hand your anxiety to God and hold on. He does not want to share the burden with us. He wants us to completely give it to Him.

A friend shared a tip with me in doing this. She said it helped her to physically act out giving her burdens to God during prayer. So, in a kneeling position, I slowly lift my clenched hands. When my arms are fully extended above my head, I open my fingers with my palms toward the sky. I have found that the actual enactment of casting my worries to God helps me release them mentally as well.

So, when worry hits, let's remember to "cast" it to our Father (1 Peter 5:7). He is in control, and He already knows the outcome. And as we know and believe this is TRUTH, just as Jesus asks in Matthew 6:27, "Which of you by taking thought can add one cubit unto his stature," how does our worry help? (KJV).

BIBLE READING: 1 PETER 5:7; MATTHEW 6:27

The Power of the Sword

"THY WORD HAVE I HID IN MINE HEART,
THAT I MIGHT NOT SIN AGAINST THEE."
PSALM 119:11 KJV

When my mother was a child, due to hardships and extenuating circumstances in her family, she and her eldest brother had to live in an orphanage for a short time. Being away from her parents and her younger siblings was traumatizing enough, but the uncertainty of when and if she would get to go home left her in an almost suffocating cloud of darkness. Yet, in that cloud of darkness, she sharpened her sword... her sword of the Spirit. Instead of allowing that cloud of fear to smother her and petrify her soul, she clung to the living Word and stored it in her heart.

The author in Psalm 119:11 says, "Thy word have I hid in mine heart, that I might not sin against thee" (KJV). And that is just what that little girl did. Instead of giving in to the whispers of loneliness penetrating her young ears, she chose to memorize scripture. She memorized Psalm 37 in its entirety and recited it again and again.

Eventually, my mother and her brother returned to their home. However, that brief time in the orphanage was only a glimpse of the many valleys my mother has walked through in her life. I use the word, 'through,' because my mother did not stay in those valleys. God brought her through them.

When I am in the valley, I may or may not be responsible for how I got there, but I can choose how I handle myself there. My mother did not choose to live in an orphanage, but she chose how she handled it. She deliberately chose to wield the sword of the Spirit, etching the TRUTH of God's Word on her heart.

Let us choose wisely today. Let's record God's Word in our minds and hearts.

Bible Reading: Psalm 119:11

No Room for Compromise

"NO MAN CAN SERVE TWO MASTERS: FOR EITHER HE WILL HATE THE ONE, AND LOVE THE OTHER; OR ELSE HE WILL HOLD TO THE ONE, AND DESPISE THE OTHER. YE CANNOT SERVE GOD AND MAMMON." MATTHEW 6:24 KJV

When my children were in elementary and middle school, we would choose a book to read together that had also been adapted into a movie. Then, once we had finished the book, we would watch the movie version as a family. My kids quickly realized that the movies were never exactly the same as the book. Some movies had left scenes out, probably because of time restraints. Another film had changed the age of the main character from a child to an older teen, which appeared to be because they wanted to add a bit of a romantic edge to the story. Believe it or not, one movie had eliminated what I had felt to be the key message conveyed in the story. Regardless of how the movie adaptation varied, the change was made because the initial book did not completely fit the parameters the movie company was looking for.

As I was thinking about various things affecting our culture today and the stresses on our young people to understand and decipher right from wrong when so many ideas are thrown at them, I have to question if we are allowing the same thing to happen with the Word of God that movie companies do when they adapt a book into a film. Instead of obeying and interpreting God's Word as it is written, we are picking, choosing, and twisting the scripture to accommodate and fit the way we want to live.

However, as children of God, we should not be adapting the Bible to fit our needs. Instead, we should be doing the opposite, seeking daily to become more like Jesus and aspiring to live in accordance with God's Word. In 2 Timothy 3:16, we are told, "All scripture is given by inspiration of God, and is profitable for doctrine, for reproof, for correction, for instruction in righteousness" (KJV). It does not say 'some scripture,' it says, 'all scripture.' And, in Romans 12:2, Paul clearly instructs, "...be not conformed to this world: but be ye transformed by the renewing of your mind, that ye may prove what is that good, and acceptable, and perfect, will of God" (KJV). If we are not adhering to all of God's Word, then we must be conforming to this world. And if we are conforming to this world, we cannot be transformed.

Let us not be conformed but transformed, striving to live according to every Word that God has given us. After all, Jesus warned in Matthew 6:24, "No man can serve two masters: for either he will hate the one, and love the other; or else he will hold to the one, and despise the other. Ye cannot serve God and mammon" (KJV).

BIBLE READING: 2 TIMOTHY 3:16; ROMANS 12:2; MATTHEW 6:24

Look At the Map

"AND NO MARVEL; FOR SATAN HIMSELF IS TRANSFORMED INTO AN ANGEL OF LIGHT. THEREFORE IT IS NO GREAT THING IF HIS MINISTERS ALSO BE TRANSFORMED AS

THE MINISTERS OF RIGHTEOUSNESS..." 2 CORINTHIANS 11:14-15 KJV

We often have problems with deliveries to our home. Apparently, some GPS apps instruct the driver to take a dirt road that ends in the middle of an open field, or the directions do not even bring them to our street, but rather to a street over from us with instructions to cut through another person's yard. However, if one looks at the map, our street is clearly there, and at the end of our drive is a large mailbox with oversized numbers marking the location.

In the Old Testament, God had given Jeremiah a message to deliver. However, Jeremiah's message was not what the people wanted to hear. They did not want to hear or believe that God was unhappy with them for their disobedience. They did not want to hear of the punishment that was coming for their lack of repentance. In Jeremiah 36, we are told that when the message Jeremiah had written down was read before King Jehoiakim, he sliced it into pieces with his knife and burned it.

- "... he cut it with the penknife and cast it into the fire that was on the hearth..." (Jeremiah 36:23 KJV).

But in Jeremiah 23, God warns of listening to false prophets delivering a feel-good message that is not from the Lord.

- "Thus saith the Lord of hosts, Hearken not unto the words of the prophets that prophesy unto you: they make you vain: they speak a vision of their own heart, and not out of the mouth of the Lord" (Jeremiah 23:16 KJV).

In life, we often come to a fork in the road where we have a decision to make. Some of these decisions are major and life-altering while others may not have so great an impact. We also hear many messages that are meant to direct us one way or another in our walk with Christ. How do we know which path to choose or what messages to accept and allow to direct us? First, we need to read God's Word daily, dig deep into the scriptures ourselves, and let His living Word speak to our hearts.

- "For the word of God is quick, and powerful, and sharper than any twoedged sword, piercing even to the dividing asunder of soul and spirit, and of the joints and marrow, and is a discerner of the thoughts and intents of the heart" (Hebrews 4:12 KJV).

Second, we need to pray. We need to go to the Father and humbly communicate with Him one-on-one constantly.

- "Be careful for nothing; but in every thing by prayer and supplication with thanksgiving let your requests be made known unto God. And the peace of God, which passeth all understanding, shall keep your hearts and minds through Christ Jesus" (Philippians 4:6-7 KJV).

Just as in Jeremiah's time, we will encounter many false teachings. In 2 Corinthians 11:14-15, we are warned, "And no marvel; for Satan himself is transformed into an angel of light. Therefore it is no great thing if his ministers also be transformed as the ministers of righteousness..."(KJV). So, we must be on guard, looking to God's Word to discern what is really from God.

As in my opening example, instead of only listening, we need to look at the map to verify the authenticity and accuracy of what we hear.

BIBLE READING: JEREMIAH 36; JEREMIAH 23:16; PHILIPPIANS 4:6-7; HEBREWS 4:12; 2 CORINTHIANS 11:14-15

Emotional Waves

"... RUN WITH PATIENCE THE RACE THAT IS SET BEFORE US." HEBREWS 12:1 KJV

The line is so long, and the longer I wait, the tighter my chest becomes and the more I tremble. I am not a thrill seeker, nor do I like roller coasters. Even though I know that the ride only lasts a minute or so and that I will be fine, the thought of being strapped in this little cart that is going to jerk my body around, lift me high, and then drop me multiple times, fills me with panic.

We finally make it through the line, and with my heart pounding so hard that I am sure others must hear it, I get strapped into the little car. My daughter asks why I am squeezing my eyes closed and gripping the bar so tight that my knuckles are white when the ride hasn't even started yet.

"Just making sure I am ready," I respond in a shaky voice. The cart takes off at warp speed, twisting and turning, then slows to a creep as it climbs and climbs and climbs, then drops faster than it took off. And when I think it must be over and start to loosen my grip, the bottom falls out for one last grand finale.

Heaving a sigh of relief, I step from the little cart. *I made it. I can relax. It's over.*

And then... I hear someone say, "Let's do it again."

Many people love amusement parks. After all, a lot of us center our vacations around going to them. Yet, I am one of those who likes to be more of a spectator when it comes to thrill-seeking. The older I get, the less I like them and the more anxious the rides make me. My adventures are found in a good Christian suspense novel (actions and thrills with my feet planted firmly on the ground).

But I share this story because when I think about life on this earth and the emotions that accompany it, the image of a roller coaster pops into my head. One minute we may be anxious about something that is upcoming, and then we are slowly climbing to great heights and the view is amazing. We reach the top, and before we can take a breath, the ground beneath us disappears, and we drop.

As I read Jeremiah 20, I am filled with that same awe as when I read the Psalms of lament. The pure human emotion flooding through the words written by someone thousands of years ago reflects the same roller coaster of emotions we experience today. At the beginning of the chapter, Jeremiah is suffering. He has been beaten for the message he is sharing. So many are prophesying lies, and Jeremiah's message is not one they want to hear or believe. But Jeremiah doesn't change his message. He continues and holds true to the words that God has given him.

However, as can be seen in the next few verses, Jeremiah's continuation is not without inner turmoil. In this emotional valley, he tells God of his distress. Jeremiah wants to stop. He doesn't want to endure the persecution anymore, yet he can't stop. He knows this is what he is called to do, and he cannot contain the message inside.

In verse 13, Jeremiah praises God. He seems to be on a mountaintop as he passionately proclaims, "Sing unto the Lord, praise ye the Lord: for he hath delivered the soul of the poor from the hand of evildoers" (Jeremiah 20:13 KJV). Then, immediately in the next verse, his emotions appear to take a nosedive again. He says, "Cursed be the day wherein I was born: let not the day wherein my mother bare me be blessed" (Jeremiah 20:14 KJV).

Our situation may be different than Jeremiah's, but the ups and downs we feel as we go through each day are not. As Christians, we are called to share the Gospel and shine for Jesus. But as our love for Jesus is so great and the desire burns within us to share what He has done, the enemy is firing darts. In 1 Peter 5:8, we are warned, "... your adversary the devil, as a roaring lion, walketh about, seeking whom he may devour" (KJV). Just as these false prophets made it hard for Jeremiah's message to be heard, the devil is working overtime, placing stumbling blocks everywhere he can. He wants to keep that message from spreading.

But, in the same way that Jeremiah continued to proclaim and fulfill God's purpose, let us "run with patience the race that is set before us" (Hebrews 12:1 KJV).

BIBLE READING: JEREMIAH 20; HEBREWS 12:1; 1 PETER 5:8

Two Out Of Twelve

"IF THE LORD DELIGHT IN US, THEN HE WILL BRING US INTO THIS LAND, AND GIVE IT US; A LAND WHICH FLOWETH WITH MILK AND HONEY." NUMBERS 14:8 KJV

Twelve men were chosen for the mission. Shammua, Shaphat, Caleb, Igal, Oshea (Joshua), Palti, Gaddiel, Gaddi, Ammiel, Sethur, Nahbi, and Geuel were going to be spies. Their assignment was to check out the land of Canaan, the Promised Land. Moses wanted to know about the land, the people, and the cities.

Forty days later, the twelve spies returned to report their findings. Overcome with fear and doubt, ten of the men detailed fortified cities and mighty giants who they had no chance of defeating. They said, "...We be not able to go up against the people; for they are stronger than we... there we saw the giants, the sons of Anak, which come of the giants: and we were in our own sight as grasshoppers, and so we were in their sight." (Numbers 13:31 & 33 KJV).

Now the other two men also witnessed the same giants and fortified cities in the land of Canaan, but they were not afraid. Instead, they were ready to go up against the giants right then. Why? Because they had unshakable faith in God. They had complete trust in Him. They said, "If the Lord delight in us, then he will bring us into this land, and give it to us; a land which floweth with milk and honey" (Numbers 14:8 KJV). Even though the Israelites may have looked like grasshoppers against the giants, Joshua and Caleb knew the giants who overshadowed them would be no more than grasshoppers to God.

As I read the details of this story in Numbers 13 and 14 this week, I couldn't help but wonder if I would have been in the group of ten, frightened and ready to bail, or would I have been a Caleb or a Joshua? Would I have let fear shut me down and keep me from following through with God's plan or would I have stood strong and faced the giants, knowing that anything is possible with God?

My self-assessment brought me to the present as I thought about the giants around me or the things that I perceive to be giants, those hurdles and obstacles that the enemy puts a magnifying glass in front of because he wants me to cower and not accomplish what God wants me to do. As much as I want to be a Caleb or a Joshua, I have to admit fear gets the best of me sometimes, and I have to remind myself that the Creator of the universe is my Heavenly Father. He knows every breath I will take. And His Word says, "Have not I commanded thee? Be strong and of a good courage; be not afraid, neither be thou dismayed: for the Lord thy God is with thee whithersoever thou goest" (Joshua 1:9 KJV). That verse always fills me with awe. *God is always with me. Always.*

Let us aspire today to have the same courage and faith as Joshua and Caleb, knowing that He is bigger than any of our giants.

Bible Reading: Joshua 1:9; Numbers 13-14

Don't Let the Sun Go Down

"BE YE ANGRY, AND SIN NOT: LET NOT THE SUN GO DOWN UPON YOUR WRATH."
EPHESIANS 4:26 KJV

She stands frozen with her eyes locked on the photo sitting on the mantle. The two little girls in the snapshot had been inseparable as children. She blinks away the tears.

"Celia, I don't understand why you don't just call her," her husband, Tom, remarks as he steps through the arched doorway into the living room.

"I'm not calling her because she is the one who wants nothing to do with me."

Tom shakes his head. "It's been ten years. Do either of you even remember why you aren't speaking to each other?"

"Apparently, I hurt her feelings when I didn't ask her to be the maid of honor at our wedding." Celia drops her gaze to the floor, and her shoulders slump. "I honestly don't know why I didn't. For some reason, I thought the maid of honor was supposed to be a close friend, not family. But Megan should have been my first choice. She wasn't only my sister. She was my best friend."

"It's not past tense. Megan still is your sister." He lets out a sigh as he drops into the armchair in front of the fireplace.

"Well, it seems that she would beg to differ. My sister boycotts every family function that I attend. I'm fairly certain that she claims to be an only child."

He rolls his eyes. "Again, don't you think ten years is a bit too long for something so petty? You know Ephesians 4:26 says, '...let not the sun go down upon your wrath.' Please call her before it's too late."

"Too late for what?" She narrows her eyes at him. "It's been ten years."

Her phone jingles in her pocket. She slides it out and lifts it to her ear. "Hey, Mom. What's going on?... Megan's been in a car accident...." Celia swallows hard as the phone trembles in her shaking hand. "Is she going to be alright?"

You may wonder why I would leave the above fictional story on a cliffhanger. My answer... I wanted to illustrate real life. We never know what the next second will hold, much less the next day. However, there is someone who does know, and that's God. And what does God tell us through scripture? His Word says, "...let not the sun go down upon your wrath." (Ephesians 4:26 KJV)

I remember watching old television shows as a child where two families had feuded for so many generations that they didn't even know the reason. The cause of the argument never got passed down... only the anger.

This week, I read the story in John 8 about the woman who had committed adultery. The scribes and Pharisees brought her to Jesus and asked, "Now Moses in the law commanded us, that such should be stoned: but what sayest thou?" (John 8:5 KJV). And of course, Jesus responded, "...He that is without sin among you, let him first cast a stone at her" (John 8:7 KJV).

Grudges and hurt feelings often destroy relationships and rip families apart. Sometimes it's something minor, and sometimes it's something major. But when God says, "...let not the sun go down," we shouldn't harbor the anger and let it build and go on and on. We need to try to fix those broken bonds immediately. I have witnessed firsthand family members and close friendships lose so much time together, and isn't that what the devil wants? John 10:10 details, "The thief cometh not, but for to steal, and to kill, and to destroy..." (KJV). And when we let anger and grudges keep us from one another, the devil is stealing our time with them.

As Jesus reminded the scribes and Pharisees that no one is without sin, let us remember that if anyone was perfect and did not make mistakes, Jesus would not have had to die and suffer on the cross. But He did. And He continuously extends forgiveness. When I make a mistake, He never turns his back on me. He is there with open arms to forgive me.

As followers of Christ, shouldn't we aspire to be more like Jesus? Let us pray together that we will treasure the time we have been given with those we love and instead of harboring grudges, we will be watching and preparing for the return of our Savior, showing and sharing His love and forgiveness with all those around us.

Bible Reading: Ephesians 4:26; John 8:5-7; John 10:10

Through the Tears

"... WEEPING MAY ENDURE FOR A NIGHT,
BUT JOY COMETH IN THE MORNING."
PSALM 30:5 KJV

Have you ever been in such anguish that you could not sleep? Have you ever laid in bed and cried all night? Have you ever shed so many tears that your eyes became swollen and sore? I know I have had a quite a few of those nights. Once, I even cried so much that one of my eyes bruised. Until then, I did not know that could happen. As humans, none of us are exempt from hard times. And depression affects many people. Both of my grandmothers suffered from it, and with my OCD, I often feel myself in a constant battle with depression. Hard times do not necessarily have to befall me to have one of those sleepless, tear-filled nights. Sometimes, it is just an overwhelming, unexplained sadness.

I often find comfort in reading the Book of Psalms, especially the Psalms of lament. I suppose it is the heartfelt connection that I feel to the emotion poured out in the words, the emotion expressing the depth and reality of human struggles. Each day, I repeat scripture out loud, and in those moments of struggle, I specifically repeat Psalm 6:6 and 9, which says, "I am weary with my groaning; all the night make I my bed to swim; I water my couch wth my tears... The Lord hath heard my supplication; the Lord will receive my prayer" (KJV).

In this scripture, David writes about the intense pain eating away at him. He pulls us into this dark place with him and allows us to identify with the intensity of his suffering. But then, David reminds us that we are not alone. He reminds us that hope is not lost because God hears our prayers. God hears our pleas for help that are intertwined with our tears. David's wording makes it clear that he is not wondering if God hears Him nor is he questioning God's presence. David is making a statement that does not contain even a hint of doubt. David is saying with complete certainty that God has heard his crying and has received his request.

So, we must remember, in our darkest moments, when the enemy wants us to think all hope is gone, God is right there collecting our tears and hearing the prayers echoing through our sobs.

"Thou tellest my wanderings: put thou my tears into thy bottle: are they not in thy book?" Psalm 56:8 KJV.

And when we have God with us, we can endure any storm.

"...weeping may endure for a night, but joy cometh in the morning." Psalm 30:5 KJV

BIBLE READING: PSALM 6; PSALM 30:5; PSALM 56:8

Molt and Move Forward

"THEREFORE IF ANY MAN BE IN CHRIST, HE IS A NEW CREATURE: OLD THINGS ARE PASSED AWAY; BEHOLD, ALL THINGS ARE BECOME NEW." 2 CORINTHIANS 5:17 KJV

Throughout our housebuilding process, we accumulated quite a few pallets and scraps of unused boards, landscaping timber, and stone, which we have stored behind the garage. The other day, my husband was digging through the pile of unused pressure-treated lumber to see if there was anything he could use in a project that he was working on. As he shifted the boards, I gasped, not in fear, but in awe at the size of the snakeskin that was outstretched and hanging over the landscaping timbers. Now, I am terrified of snakes, but I am also intrigued by nature. Since I knew the snake had to be long gone, I could not help but continue to stare and study it, fascinated at the positioning of the skin woven through some pieces of rebar sticking up like spikes out of the timbers. It was apparent the snake had rubbed against the rebar to help pull off the old skin.

A few days later during my Bible study, my thoughts returned to the snakeskin. The snake shed his skin because the old skin was too tight, and the creature needed rid of it in order to grow. When he slithered out of the old skin, he did not look back or try to carry the skin with him as a memento of all the great times he had before receiving new skin. No, he simply slithered away, free and with more room to grow.

In 2 Corinthians 5:17, Paul writes, "Therefore if any man be in Christ, he is a new creature: old things are passed away; behold, all things are become new" (KJV). Similarly, in Ephesians, 4:22-24, Paul instructs, "...put off concerning the former conversation the old man, which is corrupt according to the deceitful lusts; And be renewed in the spirit of your mind; And that ye put on the new man, which after God is created in righteousness and true holiness" (KJV).

When we accept Christ as our Savior, we are made new. We acknowledge and accept the sacrifice Jesus made. He paid the debt for our sins. We are forgiven and washed clean, with our past mistakes erased. We are given a new beginning to grow and flourish as a child of God. Just as the snake shed the old skin, so that he could grow, we must not look backward, but upward, toward Jesus. We should crave the word of God and desire to spend time with our Father daily, seeking His guidance, and striving to be who He created us to be.

BIBLE READING: 2 CORINTHIANS 5:17; EPHESIANS 4:22-24

No X-Ray Needed

"LOVE NOT THE WORLD, NEITHER THE THINGS THAT ARE IN THE WORLD. IF ANY MAN LOVE THE WORLD, THE LOVE OF THE FATHER IS NOT IN HIM." 1 JOHN 2:15 KJV

A couple of years ago while our house was still under construction, I hopped off the front door threshold to the ground where our porch is now. My ankle flipped to the side, and I took a tumble into the dirt. I thought I had only twisted my ankle, but since the swelling and bruising were so extreme the next day, I finally went to the doctor.

The doctor did an x-ray as a precaution. However, she believed it only to be a sprain as well and had already given me instructions on how to care for a sprained ankle. Yet, when the results came back from the radiologist, the x-ray revealed a cracked bone in the top of my foot. Apparently, when I landed, the bone in my foot cracked which led to my ankle rolling over and my collision with the dirt. Without the x-ray, even the doctor could not determine if it was a break or a sprain.

However, when it comes to the state of our hearts, God knows all. When Jesus returns for His children, no X-ray or technology will be required. Nothing can be hidden from the Father. In Luke 16:15, Jesus says to the Pharisees who were deriding Him, "...Ye are they which justify yourselves before men; but God knoweth your hearts: for that which is highly esteemed among men is abomination in the sight of God" (KJV).

How often do we find ourselves in situations where we have to make the choice to stand for Christ or blend with the crowd? If we truly love Christ and the Holy Spirit lives in us, how could we blend? Shouldn't Christ radiate from our hearts? In Mark 8:38, Jesus warns, "Whosoever therefore shall be ashamed of me and of my words in this adulterous and sinful generation; of him also shall the Son of man be ashamed, when He cometh in the glory of His Father with the holy angels" (KJV).

Let us stand for Jesus and shine His light. And when Jesus returns, let Him find us filled with the Holy Spirit and our hearts aglow with love for Him.

BIBLE READING: LUKE 16:15; MARK 8:38; 1 JOHN 2:15

The TRUTH Is Still There

"HEAVEN AND EARTH SHALL PASS AWAY,
BUT MY WORDS SHALL NOT PASS AWAY."
MATTHEW 24:35 KJV

I find forensic technology fascinating, so I like to watch those true crime documentary programs that detail how forensic evidence is used to solve murders. I am especially intrigued by those really old cases, the ones that have grown cold, and then for some reason or another, a detective comes along and decides to dig a little deeper. Then, forensic technology discovers a microscopic fiber or trace of DNA on a piece of evidence from the crime scene that has been stored away for years. And suddenly a perpetrator who thought he/she had

thoroughly disposed of any evidence all those years ago and
had gotten away with murder is finally brought to justice.

In the book of Jeremiah, chapter 36, God tells Jeremiah to
write down the words He had spoken to him concerning the
judgments that God was bringing upon these people because
they had continued to turn from God and refused to repent of
their evil ways. When the message that Jeremiah had written
down is read before King Jehoiakim, the king slices it into
pieces with his knife and burns it.

But just like the perpetrator in my example above thought
he/she had gotten rid of any incriminating evidence, the truth
was still there.

King Jehoiakim might have burned the page with the message... but the TRUTH in the words... GOD'S WORDS... was
still there. Destroying the message did not erase the judgment
that was coming. (Also note that in Jeremiah 36:28, after the
king burned the first message, God tells Jeremiah to write it
down again.)

I can't help but wonder what the king was thinking as he cut
the message into bits and tossed it into the fire. Did he think
getting rid of the written words would change what was to
come?

And then, I thought of our society today. We have God's
Word. We cannot slice, dice, and pick which parts of the Bible

we want to believe or adhere to. The Bible in its entirety is the Word of God. We know that Jesus will return for God's children, and we know that judgment will come along with the consequences of choosing not to accept Him as Savior and Lord.

Ignoring or altering the message will not change the outcome.

The TRUTH is still there. We can close our eyes and turn our heads, but the TRUTH is still there.

In Matthew 6:24, Jesus says, "No man can serve two masters: for either he will hate the one, and love the other; or else he will hold to the one, and despise the other...," and in Matthew 12:30, He warns, "He that is not with me is against me..." (KJV).

Just as we cannot go right and left simultaneously, we cannot follow the world and Jesus.

CHOOSE JESUS.

BIBLE READING: JEREMIAH 36; MATTHEW 6:24; MATTHEW 12:30

Yearn to Learn

"ALL SCRIPTURE IS GIVEN BY INSPIRATION OF GOD, AND IS PROFITABLE FOR DOCTRINE, FOR REPROOF, FOR CORRECTION, FOR INSTRUCTION IN RIGHTEOUSNESS." 2 TIMOTHY 3:16 KJV

A while back, I was approached by a young man who wanted to share with me why he did not believe the Bible to be true. He said he had been raised in a Christian home and in church, but at some point along the way, he had lost his faith. I listened as this young man explained his stance, and then he, respectfully and with an open mind, listened as I shared my faith, even taking one of my bookmarks as he left... not because he had changed his mind at that point, but because he said... "I had listened to him."

I know without a doubt that the Bible is truth. Yet, sometimes I struggle in verbal situations and wish I could better express what my heart and soul long to share. But I continue to pray that God will use me to share His message and not let me mess up the opportunities He has given me to plant a seed. And through my prayers, I've felt led to read and study more of the Old Testament. I have never enjoyed learning about history, but as I have been digging into the books of Jeremiah, Daniel, and now Ezra, I have found myself fascinated at how these books overlap and yearning to explore the exact events and timeframe of everything happening. At the heart of it all, I am astounded at the concrete evidence of the Bible's truth confirmed through the fulfilled prophecy contained in these books.

In 2 Timothy 3:16, we are told, "All scripture is given by inspiration of God, and is profitable for doctrine, for reproof, for correction, for instruction in righteousness" (KJV). In the last few weeks, through the enormous amount of understanding that I have gained by not just reading but actually studying these books, I have realized the importance and the need to spend time with the Word of God each day. Not only have I grown closer to God and added to my spiritual armor, but I am better equipped to share the Gospel. After all, in the book of Acts, could Philip have explained the scripture to the man in the chariot, if he had not read and studied it himself?

"And Philip ran thither to him, and heard him read the prophet Esaias, and said, Understandest thou what thou readest? And he said, How can I, except some man should guide me? And he desired Philip that he would come up and sit with him.... Then Philip opened his mouth, and began at the same scripture, and preached unto him Jesus." Acts 8:30-31, 35 KJV

BIBLE READING: 2 TIMOTHY 3:16; ACTS 8:26-40

Faith That Holds

"NOW FAITH IS THE SUBSTANCE OF THINGS HOPED FOR, THE EVIDENCE OF THINGS NOT SEEN." HEBREW 11:1 KJV

My grandmother passed away about twenty-five years ago. However, I still have a lot of vivid memories of her, and the majority of them revolve around her faith. In my earliest memories, I was about five years old. I would stay a few hours at a time with my grandparents while my mom worked or ran errands. It was an older house, so in order to get to the bathroom that had been a later addition, I had to walk through the bedroom. In all the times that I passed through that bedroom, I never recollect seeing my grandmother's Bible closed. It was always lying open on her bed.

In later memories, my mother and I lived with my grandmother for a bit. I was around twelve years old, and during that time of sharing her residence, my grandmother was either listening to Christian radio, watching a message on a Christian network on television, or talking about God. And, again, her Bible was always open.

Now that I am older, I have often thought about my grandmother and the tough life that she endured. I have often asked myself how she coped. It seemed the enemy wreaked nonstop havoc in her life. She went from enduring an abusive relationship early in her life to losing a son to suicide to, later on, losing her husband the same way, and then on to her other son spending time incarcerated because of bad choices linked to alcoholism. While I cannot fathom as a wife and mother having to face any one of these things, she had to cope with them all.

So, as I ask myself how she did it, I know it had to be her shield of faith. Paul lists the shield of faith along with its purpose in the armor of God. In Ephesians 6:16, he says, "Above all, taking the shield of faith, wherewith ye shall be able to quench all the fiery darts of the wicked" (KJV).

Hebrews 11:1 defines faith. "Now faith is the substance of things hoped for, the evidence of things not seen" (KJV). My grandmother believed with her whole heart that Jesus died for her sins and that this life was temporary. And she knew without a doubt that one day, He would wipe away her tears, and there would be no more pain.

BIBLE READING: EPHESIANS 6:16; HEBREWS 11:1

It Wasn't Me

"FOR ALL HAVE SINNED, AND COME SHORT OF THE GLORY OF GOD." ROMANS 3:23 KJV

*I*t wasn't me. It wasn't my fault...

I suppose one could conclude that passing the blame is part of our sinful nature. After all, when confronted by God in the garden, Adam, in a sense, pointed his finger at Eve, and Eve, in a sense, pointed her finger at the snake.

"And the man said, The woman whom thou gavest to be with me, she gave me of the tree, and I did eat. ...And the woman said, The serpent beguiled me, and I did eat." Genesis 3:12-13 KJV

But as my father-in-law used to say, when you point your finger at someone else, there are three pointing back at yourself. And if you try it, you will see that it is true. If I point my index finger away from me, my other three fingers are pointing back toward me.

That said, as I read Daniel's prayer in chapter nine, I was taken aback by his genuine humility. Here is a man who diligently prayed and remained faithful to God no matter the consequences. Yet, as he prayed, confessing the sins of Israel and asking for God's mercy on them, he used the word, 'we.' He did not point his finger nor did he say, 'it wasn't me, God.' Instead, Daniel included himself in confessing the sin of Israel, even though he had remained faithful to his Creator. Why?

Romans 3:23 reminds us that "...all have sinned, and come short of the glory of God" (KJV).

I believe Daniel knew that even though he had not taken part in the disobedience that had brought on God's wrath, he was still not deserving of God's mercy. Therefore, he did not point fingers and cast blame. On the contrary, he came to God with humility, seeking the grace that none of us deserve but all need.

Let us follow Daniel's example, not casting blame or passing judgment, but rather humbly bowing in prayer to our Father who loves us enough to extend mercy and grace that we do not deserve.

BIBLE READING: DANIEL 9; ROMANS 3:23; GENESIS 3:12-13

Do Others See Jesus in Me?

"LET YOUR LIGHT SO SHINE BEFORE MEN, THAT THEY MAY SEE YOUR GOOD WORKS, AND GLORIFY YOUR FATHER WHICH IS IN HEAVEN." MATTHEW 5:16 KJV

Living in a land where they were surrounded by idolatry and a law that should have forced them to conform to the world around them, Shadrach, Meshach, and Abednego refused to compromise their faith. King Nebuchadnezzar had created a golden idol, and when the music played, all were required to fall and worship his statue. They could have avoided adversity. They could have pretended to worship. But if they had, they would have hidden their love for God, and how could others know about the true God if their lives were not examples for Him. However, in the same way, they did not flaunt or seek attention for their disobedience of the law. They did not shout in the street and stir trouble. They simply did not conform. They continued to worship only God and others saw. Some became angry and told the king. Yet, upon confrontation, literally in the heat of the moment, they stood strong with character and dignity, proclaiming their obedience only to God.

As many times as I have heard the story of Shadrach, Meshach, and Abednego in Daniel, chapter 3, I had never really thought about how they did not flaunt their disobedience to the king. However, they followed and remained faithful to God and others saw.

I realized this was a prime example of how our lives are a testament for Christ. When we say that we are Christians, others are watching and viewing us as representatives of Jesus.

The question is, when others watch and listen, do they see and hear the love of a devoted follower of Christ? Do the things we say and do lead people to Christ or push them away?

Quite a while ago, my family relocated to the northern states. We lived in Maine for two years. Now having been born and raised in the South, my speech was a dead giveaway that my roots were not local. Everywhere I went, people would ask where I was from.

As I think of how obvious my dialect was to others and how they knew as soon as I spoke that I was not from that area, shouldn't my love for Jesus be just as obvious? If I am with friends or family, at the store, or in a restaurant, would others wonder or need to ask if I am a Christian? Do my actions and words reflect the love of Christ?

Do others see Jesus in me?

BIBLE READING: DANIEL 3; MATTHEW 5:16

The ONE Who Understands

"... For He hath said, I will never leave thee, nor forsake thee." Hebrews 13:5 KJV

"But then, I think of the rejection and the scars on His hands,
And I curl up in the arms of the One who understands.
I cling to Him and His promise of the coming day,
When I will have no more tears, and the pain will go away.
I'm not alone... I'm not alone.
He will never leave me. I'm not alone."

Have you ever felt as if the devil was attacking so hard in your state of weakness that you could not endure? Have you ever sat alone heartbroken and in tears? Have you ever been failed by someone close to you or your trust betrayed by a friend? Have you ever had one of those heart-pounding, sweat-soaked, panic-ridden moments? Have you ever felt like no one could possibly understand what you are going through?

The opening poem is an excerpt from my novel, *NEVER FORGET THE TRUTH*. One of the characters, Ellie, is in an ultimate battle with the enemy. In her broken state, she sings these lyrics to remind herself that she is not alone and that there is One who truly does understand and can empathize with her suffering.

And while my novel is fiction, the One who understands is real. And, God's Word reveals and details much about how Jesus really does understand.

Jesus understands temptation, even in a state of weakness. After all, Jesus was tested by Satan himself, and not under conditions where a person would be at one's strongest, but after fasting for forty days. Matthew 4:1-2 states, "Then was Jesus led up of the Spirit into the wilderness to be tempted of the devil. And when he had fasted forty days and forty nights, he was afterward an hungred" (KJV). I, honestly, cannot imagine how weak He must have been physically and mentally. If I skip breakfast and lunch, by afternoon, not only do I feel physically sick but my mind is foggy and I have difficulty focusing on a task. Yet, Jesus had fasted for forty days.

Jesus understands heartbreak.

After Lazarus died, Jesus wept when he saw Mary. John 11:33-35 details, "When Jesus therefore saw her weeping, and the Jews also weeping which came with her, he groaned in the spirit, and was troubled. And said, Where have ye laid him? They said unto him, Lord, come and see. Jesus wept" (KJV). Jesus was troubled by Mary's pain. The verse does not say, but I believe Jesus is weeping in response to Mary's hurting heart and not because of the death of his friend. Jesus loves Lazarus, but He also knows He is going to raise him and Lazarus will live.

Jesus understands being let down by those closest to us.

Jesus knew what lay ahead for Him. Jesus told his closest friends how He felt as He said to them, "...My soul is exceeding sorrowful, even unto death: tarry ye here and watch with me" (Matthew 26:38 KJV). After Jesus prays, he returns and, "...findeth them asleep..." (Matthew 26:40 KJV).

Jesus understands betrayal.

After all, in exchange for money ("... thirty pieces of silver"), it was one of Jesus' friends who turned Him over to the authorities (Matthew 26:15 KJV). We know that not only was Judas one of Jesus' disciples, but Jesus thought of him as a friend. In Matthew 26:50, when Judas led the authorities to Jesus, Jesus said to Judas, "...Friend, wherefore art thou come?..." (KJV).

Jesus understands anxiety and stress.

Jesus knew His purpose in coming to earth as a man. He knew what He would have to endure. But yet, He came. And we know from previous examples, that He felt emotional pain. He wept and felt sorrow. But also in the garden, as He prayed, we are given a vivid image of His stress level. Luke 22:44 describes the scene by saying, "And being in an agony he prayed more earnestly: and his sweat was as it were great drops of blood falling to the ground" (KJV).

There is One Who understands, and He promises never to betray us or leave us alone. The scripture clearly states, "...for He hath said, I will never leave thee, nor forsake thee" (Hebrews 13:5 KJV).

BIBLE READING: HEBREWS 13:5; MATTHEW 4:1-2; JOHN 11:33-35; MATTHEW 26:15, 38-50; LUKE 22:44

Stand Out

"*YE ARE THE LIGHT OF THE WORLD. A CITY THAT IS SET ON A HILL CANNOT BE HID.*"
MATTHEW 5:14 KJV

After we poured the concrete porch at our new house, we still did not have the yard or sidewalk complete. To keep from ruining our new porch with muddy footprints, we laid cardboard across it, forming a walkway to the door. That's when Leonard moved in. This bright green lizard set up residence under the cardboard, and we had to be careful when stepping on the cardboard for fear of crushing him. However, on warm days walking on the cardboard was safe because Leonard came out to soak up the heat from the sun. And because of his vibrant, almost neon green color against the gray concrete, he stood out like a white turkey in the woods. I'm guessing Leonard was meant to live in trees or shrubbery where his color would have blended with the leaves, camouflaging him from an adversary. Be that as it may, Leonard did not choose to blend in. Instead, he stood out.

In Matthew 5:14-16, Jesus says, "Ye are the light of the world. A city that is set on an hill cannot be hid. Neither do men light a candle, and put it under a bushel, but on a candlestick; and it giveth light unto all that are in the house. Let your light so shine before men, that they may see your good works, and glorify your Father which is in heaven" (KJV). God's Word commands us to be a light for Him. And in this world that keeps growing darker, any kind of light will be highly visible, just like a bright green lizard on a concrete porch.

So, I have to stop and ask myself. *Am I like the bright green lizard making a daily choice to stand out for Christ in a dark world, or do I blend with the darkness around me in fear of persecution?*

In Romans 12:2 (KJV), Paul states, "...be not conformed to this world...," and in Philippians 2:14-16, he instructs us to, "Do all things without murmurings and disputings: That ye may be blameless and harmless, the sons of God, without rebuke, in the midst of a crooked and perverse nation, among whom ye shine as lights in the world; Holding forth the word of life; that I may rejoice in the day of Christ, that I have not run in vain, neither laboured in vain" (KJV).

God's Word is clear. We should not blend like a green lizard on a green leaf in fear of what others will think of us or afraid of being persecuted for our faith. Instead, we are to be a light in the darkness, letting our lives radiate the love of Jesus. But how?

We don't make choices that compromise our faith. Instead, we follow God's instructions for our lives and reflect our faith in everything we do. We don't just say we are followers of Jesus. We show that we are followers of Jesus.

Matthew 5:14 specifically uses the words, "...a city on a hill..." (KJV). And of course, it takes a group of people to make up a city. As the family of God, we need to come together and be that city on the hill, a city that is so brightly lit that our children and all those around us can see their way to Jesus. Let's be like Leonard and choose to stand out. After all, we can't complain about the darkness, if we don't make an effort to light it up.

BIBLE READING: MATTHEW 5:14-16; ROMANS 12:2; PHILIPPIANS 2:14-16

Rich Without Measure

"I COUNSEL THEE TO BUY OF ME GOLD TRIED IN THE FIRE, THAT THOU MAYEST BE RICH..."
REVELATION 3:18 KJV

I know that I am not the only one frustrated by rising prices. Groceries, gas, you name it..., and the price has increased. Now that my children are older and have had the experience of working and paying for some things themselves, they are starting to realize how expensive it is to live in this world. I remember my daughter having a project to do for an economics class. She had to create a budget for her finances according to where she planned to live and the career path she intended to follow. When her project was complete, she had concluded that she did not know how she was going to be able to afford to be an adult. And when gas prices surged a few years ago, my son who had been driving for a bit suddenly decided that he "really enjoyed going places with his mother." Now that he is away at college and having to purchase some groceries, he no longer has any complaints about using the store brand instead of the name brand.

Of course, money is required to pay for basic needs, but if I am honest, how much money do I spend on things that are not a necessity? For instance, my phone makes my life easier. It tells me how to get from place to place. I can compare prices when I am in the middle of a store. I can check product reviews. I can see where my children are. But my phone is not a necessary expense, and I did just fine before cell phones existed.

No matter what we buy with it, our world revolves around money, and I am quite sure everyone wants to feel financially secure.

But does an abundance of money really make a person happy?

King Solomon shares in Ecclesiastes that those who desire money will never have enough. In Ecclesiastes 5:10 and 12, he states, "He that loveth silver shall not be satisfied with silver; nor he that loveth abundance with increase: this is also vanity. ...The sleep of a labouring man is sweet, whether he eat little or much: but the abundance of the rich will not suffer him to sleep" (KJV).

So, what is real treasure?

God's Word tells us we should focus on our treasure in Heaven. In Matthew 6:20, Jesus instructs, "... lay up for yourselves treasures in heaven, where neither moth nor rust doth corrupt, and where thieves do not break through nor steal" (KJV). In the end, the worldly riches we accumulate will be destroyed. After all, our time on this earth is only temporary. We have so many financial plans available to help us prepare for retirement, but our first concern should be investing in our eternal home.

Finally, look at these instructions found in scripture on how to be rich. Revelation 3:18 says, "I counsel thee to buy of me gold tried in the fire, that thou mayest be rich..." (KJV). And where do we get this gold tried in the fire? This is also revealed to us in the scripture. In 1 Peter 1:7, we are told, "That the trial of your faith, being much more precious than of gold that perisheth, though it be tried by fire, might be found unto praise and honour and glory at the appearing of Jesus Christ" (KJV). If gold is purified in the fire, then our faith is purified in the trials of life. As we purify our faith, withstanding the tests and trials by trusting and clinging to our Father, our treasure increases because our faith becomes stronger.

So, our belief in Christ makes us rich... rich beyond measure.

BIBLE READING: ECCLESIASTES 5:10-12; MATTHEW 6:20; REVELATION 3:18; 1 PETER 1:7

A Safe Haven

"COME UNTO ME, ALL YE THAT LABOUR AND ARE HEAVY LADEN, AND I WILL GIVE YOU REST." MATTHEW 11:28 KJV

An enormous number of deer inhabit our property. The other day, a delivery driver made a comment about how the deer roam in the open so comfortably even in the midst of hunting season. This morning, as I peered out my window at this majestic doe standing by the back steps, I began to think about this person's words regarding hunting. First, let me say that I have no problem with hunting as long as the animals' meat is used for food and their lives are not taken purely for sport. However, I love gazing at the deer from the window or the porch, so I do not want hunting on my property. I treasure how safe the animals feel. If they felt threatened, I would not have the blessing of watching them. And doesn't everything deserve a safe place?

That is the beauty of having a personal relationship with Jesus. Satan is "...going to and fro in the earth..." (Job 1:7 KJV), and like a hunter in pursuit of game, Satan is like "... a roaring lion, walketh about, seeking whom he may devour" (1 Peter 5:8 KJV). The devil is always trying to make us stumble and fall. He is always trying to pull us down physically and mentally. He is always trying to take our focus off of God. But in the midst of the attack, I can open my Bible or kneel to pray, and I am in my safe haven. All of the chaos becomes background noise. The blustery wind, the pummeling hail, and the pounding waves swirl around me, yet I do not feel any of it. My time with God is a place of rest. *"Come unto me, all ye that labour and are heavy laden, and I will give you rest" (Matthew 11:28 KJV)*. My time with God fills me with a peace that passes understanding. *"And the peace of God, which passeth all understanding, shall keep your hearts and minds through Christ Jesus" (Philippians 4:7 KJV)*. It is not an emotion that can be experienced anywhere else except in the presence of the Lord. "... in thy presence is fulness of joy..." (Psalm 16:11 KJV).

I cannot imagine having non-stop chaos without being able to escape and talk to Jesus. If you do not have that safe haven, Jesus is standing with open arms. Accept His embrace. Because of His scars, we can come into His presence and find rest spending time with Him.

BIBLE READING: MATTHEW 11:28; PSALM 16:11; PHILIPPIANS 4:7; 1 PETER 5:8; JOB 1:7

When You Know it's from God

*"I SOUGHT THE LORD, AND HE HEARD ME,
AND DELIVERED ME FROM ALL MY FEARS."
PSALM 34:4 KJV*

A crumpled sticky note...
        tossed to the ground...
            picked up by a fourth grader...
                who gave it to a teacher.

T he other day I received these words from a friend. She then told me the story of a teacher she knew who had been discouraged and struggling from many difficult days. This teacher had needed a word from God, and she received a note with the exact message she needed. A student had found a crumpled sticky note on the ground, brought it into the class, and gave it to the teacher. When the teacher looked at the note, she saw the handwritten words, *I sought the Lord, and he heard me, and delivered me from all my fears. Psalm 34:4.*

As I thought about this story, the words from Psalm 139:1-4 filled my mind:

"O lord, thou hast searched me, and known me. Thou knowest my downsitting and mine uprising, thou understandest my thought afar off. Thou compassest my path and my lying down, and art acquainted with all my ways. For there is not a word in my tongue, but, lo, O Lord, thou knowest it altogether." (KJV)

Our Father knows our hearts. He knows our thoughts, and He knows our needs. Even when we are at a loss for words and do not know what to pray for, He hears the cries of our innermost being. And He gives us what we need at the precise moment we need it most. His timing is always perfect.

How often have I known without a doubt that a song, a message on the radio, or a phone call from a friend was the very voice of God speaking to me?

When my daughter was a newborn, and my son was barely a toddler, my anxiety had gone through the roof, literally. I was so frightened that I would not be able to protect them, and my fear had gotten to the point that I was not sleeping. My fear had triggered my OCD, and worry consumed every particle of my brain every minute of my day. I had been a stay-at-home mom for two years. But, prior to my son being born, there was a certain teaching broadcast that I would listen to on the radio every evening on my way home from work. Given that I no longer commuted to work, it had been quite a while (several years) since I had heard the broadcast and did not even know if it still came on.

However, one morning I had to go to the store, which would usually kick my anxiety into overdrive because I would be toting a newborn and a toddler into a germ-filled crowded environment. As I pulled out of my driveway, I flipped on the radio, and that very program, the one I had listened to several years before on my evening drive home from work, was on in the middle of the morning hours... not late evening when I had listened before. And I will give you a guess as to the topic. Yes, it was all about worry... better yet... it was about not worrying. I still get chills when I think about it because I knew that with the timing of this radio program and the message that it proclaimed... there was no other explanation. This was a message from God that, after battling months and months of this anxiety, finally gave me peace, that peace that passes understanding.

Just as He knew the teacher's need, and answered, God had heard my need, and answered.

He knows... and He will provide. We just need to seek Him.

"I sought the Lord, and he heard me, and delivered me from all my fears." Psalm 34:4 KJV

BIBLE READING: PSALM 34:4; PSALM 139:1-4

Strong Enough to be Meek

"BLESSED ARE THE MEEK: FOR THEY SHALL INHERIT THE EARTH." MATTHEW 5:5 KJV

Both my children were young when we got our Boxer puppy, Lucy. The three of them grew up together, and throughout those years, my kids played with that dog nonstop, as if she were their sibling. Lucy has been dressed up in an array of costumes and has had the pleasure of being a patient in their pretend dental office. She has had tea parties, her nails painted, and bows on her ears... all things I am sure our dog loved. I say that with a hint of sarcasm, but honestly, she probably did love it because she loved any and all attention from my children. But if she had not wanted to be dressed up as a princess or have her teeth cleaned by my children, she did not have to. Lucy was a seventy-pound boxer dog that obviously had the physical strength to object to anything that she did not want to do. But she didn't, and she wouldn't. She was meek. She was physically strong enough, but she chose to submit to my children.

In Matthew 5:5, Jesus says, "Blessed are the meek: for they shall inherit the earth" (KJV)

Meek does not indicate weakness but rather exhibits strength. Weakness is when a person cannot do something. Meekness is when a person is strong enough but chooses not to. For example, a meek person would choose not to ride the bumper of the car that just pulled out in front of him/her. They have the ability, but they choose not to.

Of course, Jesus is the perfect example of meek. He didn't have to be nailed to a cross. He didn't have to tolerate people spitting on him. He didn't have to withstand the beatings. He certainly had the power to stop any one of these things. But He allowed them to nail Him to the cross. He allowed them to mock Him and spit on Him and beat Him. He submitted to His Father's will and died in our place.

If we want to be more like Jesus, we have to be meek. We must willingly submit to God and His authority. We need to choose to relinquish control and trust God's will completely. Psalm

37:11 says, "... the meek shall inherit the earth; and shall delight themselves in the abundance of peace" (KJV).

BIBLE READING: PSALM 37:11; MATTHEW 5:5

It May Storm... But the Son Is Always There

"BUT AS FOR YOU, YE THOUGHT EVIL AGAINST ME; BUT GOD MEANT IT UNTO GOOD, TO BRING TO PASS, AS IT IS THIS DAY, TO SAVE MUCH PEOPLE ALIVE." GENESIS 50:20 KJV

L ast Monday got off to a rocky start. I woke up intending to get the laundry over with first thing. And I did get the laundry done, it just did not go exactly as I had anticipated. The washing machine suddenly decided it no longer wanted to enter the spin cycle. So, it continued to rinse and drain, rinse and drain, rinse and drain. As it repeated this process, it also reset the timer to the beginning of the rinse cycle. Needless to say, I was frustrated. I had a load of sopping wet towels that needed to be rung out before I could put them in the dryer and a list of chores that I had thought I would already have completed at this point.

However, when my husband pulled the washing machine away from the wall to work on it, he found a problem that could have turned out much worse than just a washing machine that was not spinning. A portion of the black rubber hose that connects the water supply from the house to the washing machine was swollen up like a water balloon.

Now, while a broken washing machine may have been frustrating, it could have been much worse. As my husband pointed out, if the washing machine had not torn up, we would not have found the hose that was about to burst. And if that hose had burst while we were gone, our entire house could have flooded.

What's my point? My point is that the broken washing machine actually turned out to be a blessing.

As we go through each day, we will face obstacles. Things will not always go perfectly. But God is always in control. Romans 8:28 assures, "And we know that all things work together for good to them that love God, to them who are the called according to his purpose" (KJV). Even though we only want sunshine and rainbows, if we trust Him, he will use the rain and the storms of life for good.

For example, Joseph's brothers had bad intentions. They sold Joseph as a slave and he was taken far from his home and family. He was even imprisoned for something he did not do. But in the end, his family would have starved if those bad things had not happened. In Genesis 50:20, Joseph recognized God's purpose in the storm as he said, "But as for you, ye thought evil against me; but God meant it unto good, to bring to pass, as it is this day, to save much people alive" (KJV).

In Acts 16, we are told that Paul and Silas were beaten and thrown into prison. Yet, if they had not been in prison and if they had not chosen to stay when the prison doors opened and their stocks fell off, the prison guard would not have come to know Christ that night. And if that prison guard had not come to know Christ that night, his family would not have either.

Acts 16:33-34 details, "And he took them the same hour of the night, and washed their stripes; and was baptized, he and all his, straightway. And when he had brought them into his house, he set meat before them, and rejoiced, believing in God with all his house" (KJV).

Often when we face difficulties, we find ourselves complaining and grumbling. However, as we walk with God and aspire to be more like Jesus, let us give thanks in the bad times and the good times because we know God is working things out for the good. The purpose of the storm may not be as obvious as my washing machine example. We may not see the reason right away, or we may never see the purpose in the difficulty. But we trust the God who already knows the road ahead. He may just be veering us around a giant sinkhole.

BIBLE READING: ROMANS 8:28; GENESIS 50:20; ACTS 16

The World May Be Changing... BUT...

"FOR I AM THE LORD, I CHANGE NOT..."
MALACHI 3:6 KJV

I remember as I was growing up, I often heard my parents and grandparents use the phrase, "When I was your age...." And then, I found myself using that same phrase when talking to my own children. To be honest, I still catch myself saying those words even now that they are older. But the truth is that a lot of things have changed since I was their age.

What has changed since you were in school? If you are a student, what have you heard your parents say has changed? Here are a few changes that I can easily note:

- We had no cell phones. Our school lobby had a pay phone, which at one time cost a dime but increased later to a quarter.

- We did not have laptops provided by our school. We did not have laptops at all. We brought pencils and paper... and wrote in cursive.

- We did not have a computer class. We had a typing class... on typewriters. We had computers at our school, but there were very few. It was a special occasion for a class to go to the computer lab.

- We had to go to the library for sources to use for our essays (which were handwritten). If it was a journal article, one might have to use microfiche to view it. (There was no typing a topic into a search engine in the comfort of your home and immediately have the information at your fingertips.)

- We did not have a guard, a police officer, or a metal detector at our school. (And yes, I attended public high school).

- We were still assigned lockers.

- Since we did not have cell phones, texting while driving was not an issue. The dial on the radio, cassette tapes, and later, compact discs were our distracting enemy.

- Normal network television programming did not require ratings nor did video games. My earlier televisions had a dial that only went up to thirteen. Later the cable company provided a box that connected to the television allowing for a few more channels.

- We could carry a backpack or a purse into a school ballgame without it having to be small and transparent (clear).

- We wrote checks or paid in cash... fast food did not accept cards... and, well, again paying with your phone was not an option.

- We had no social media. We talked to each other on a landline phone. (We had cordless phones... but most people still had the curly wire, so your location was pretty much stationary as long as you were talking on the phone.)

- I am not sure if a teacher in a public school now would be able to do this, but I had a teacher who asked if anyone would be offended if he read the Bible each morning aloud. No one opposed, so he did.

Obviously, a lot more has changed than the things on my list (such as prices), but my point is our world is constantly changing. In my opinion, and as a Christian, many of the changes have not been for the better. In my opinion, we are allowing the devil to gain more and more access into our homes through the content that is contained in the programming and through our technological devices that are a window to... anything and everything. While the devil only needs a crack in the door in which to stick his foot, I believe that we have made it quite easy for him and just opened a gate.

Now, don't get me wrong. I am not saying that all of the progress we have made is bad. Our children have unlimited educational resources at their fingertips. In the event of sickness or other necessary instances, work and school can be done from home. In addition, health and medical advancements offer so much more in wellness and early detection of diseases.

On top of all that, technology is a wonderful avenue to share the Gospel. We can reach so many people right from our computers.

However, in spite of all the changes, all of the technology, and all of the progress, ... God remains the same. His love remains the same. His word remains the same. His instructions for our lives remain the same. And His free gift of salvation remains the same and is still available.

Our world may have changed, but God has not.

- "Jesus Christ the same yesterday, and to day, and for

ever." Hebrews 13:8 KJV

- "For I am the Lord, I change not..." Malachi 3:6 KJV

- "The grass withereth, the flower fadeth: but the word of our God shall stand for ever." Isaiah 40:8 KJV

BIBLE READING: HEBREWS 13:8; MALACHI 3:6; ISAISH 40:8

I Didn't Ask

"WHEREAS YE KNOW NOT WHAT SHALL BE ON THE MORROW. FOR WHAT IS YOUR LIFE? IT IS EVEN A VAPOUR, THAT APPEARETH FOR A LITTLE TIME, AND THEN VANISHETH AWAY." JAMES 4:14 KJV

The burden weighs like a concrete block sitting on my chest, and panic builds inside me. My airway constricts at the thought of bringing up the topic, but I know I cannot rest until I do. Squeezing my eyes closed, I take a deep breath, attempting to calm myself and let it out slowly. *Enough procrastinating,* I pick up the phone, reminding myself of how important this is. *I need to find a way to ask him today. No! I have to find a way to ask him today!*

As my trembling finger taps the numbers on the screen, I recite in my mind what I am going to say. With every ring, the words I have rehearsed get more and more jumbled in my head, and when he answers, the words vanish. I try to think fast, but I cannot even recall the first word of the first line in my speech. *Why didn't I write it down?*

Shaking my head in frustration at myself, I sit quietly and let him talk. He immediately informs me that he has gotten his flu shot and instructs me to get mine soon. Then, I listen as he tells me of his latest self-diagnosis and how he no longer has diabetes. I listen as he complains about the lack of work in the small town where he lives. I listen as he talks about politics, the economy, and how everything is getting worse. I listen as he reminisces about the time President Kennedy spent in office.

Of course, we only scratch the surface of these topics. Our conversations never get too personal. A wall stands in the way of the connection that we should share. Our blood could not be of more relation, and our mannerisms match in more ways than either of us would ever admit. However, circumstances voided the bond between us early in my life. Unfortunately, we were only able to rebuild superficial ties, and we converse as if we are nothing more than acquaintances. I love him dearly, and I know that he feels the same. We just cannot break through that awkward barrier that allows us to express it.

My mind drifts away from the cacophony of his political speech as a voice deep inside keeps distracting me. Over and over, the phrase "just ask him" repeats, but I can't. I am afraid that he will get angry. *Why would he get mad?* I question, trying to reassure myself. *Well, if he doesn't get mad, I might hurt his feelings. He probably expects me to know.* I drop my head. *But I don't know.* For years I have pretended that I know, but in reality, I am ashamed to say that I don't, not for sure anyway, and that's not good enough.

When I was a little girl, we would go to church. Back then, I remember him saying he was saved and that he had even been baptized, but I never recollect seeing him pray. For that matter, other than his recitation of the verses about wives submitting to their husbands and children obeying their parents, I do not remember him reading his Bible. And now that I am older, well, he never even mentions his faith.

As I hold the phone to my ear, my stomach twists into knots. The conviction to ask him sends a pang through my heart, but fear will not let the words escape my lips. I try to make excuses. I make every effort to convince myself that he would not be honest anyway, but that does not silence the voice nagging from within. Pushing the anxiety down, I force myself from my thoughts and snap my attention back to the conversation.

Oh, brother! He is still rambling about the election. All of a sudden, I have an idea that might break the ice and give me a chance to read his reaction. I wait for him to take a breath so I can get a word in, and when the moment finally comes, I rattle the question off so fast that I don't even hear the words come out. "Is Grandma a Christian?"

"What?" his voice reflects surprise. I suppose my inquiry is a little off the topic at hand.

Great. Now I have to repeat myself. "Grandma. She is getting older, and it has me worried. Do you know if she has accepted Jesus? I want to know for sure that she is going to Heaven."

"Oh, well, she... that's just... just something you never really know about another person...," he chokes out, then pauses for a second before he continues. "But anyway, who do you think is going to win the election?"

I swallow the lump in my throat and try to pretend that I know something about politics.

I never worked up the nerve to approach the subject again, and I no longer have the opportunity. Less than a year after this phone conversation, he passed away at the age of sixty-four from a heart attack.

I cling to the childhood memory of him taking our family to church. I cling to his Bible engraved with his name. I cling to a picture with the lyrics of "Amazing Grace" displayed on his wall. I cling to these items hoping he had a personal relationship with Jesus.

I have learned firsthand that tomorrow is not guaranteed. For that matter, the next minute is not guaranteed. I have learned firsthand that I may not get a second chance to tell another person about Jesus, so I better seize every opportunity.

Today, let us not miss an opportunity to tell someone about Jesus.

BIBLE READING: JAMES 4:14

Tunnel Vision

"Not that I speak in respect of want: for I have learned, in whatsoever state I am, therewith to be content."
Philippians 4:11 KJV

P icture the scene. The sun is shining. The birds are singing. Large colorful flowers dot their midst, and enormous trees with humongous fruit surround them. Adam and Eve can eat all they want of any of the fruit from any of the trees except one. God tells them in Genesis 2:16-17, "And the Lord God commanded the man, saying, Of every tree of the garden thou mayest freely eat: But of the tree of the knowledge of good and evil, thou shalt not eat of it..." (KJV).

So, what's the problem?

Let me recap. Sunshine, flowers, trees, singing birds, amazing animals, and all they can eat anytime their heart desires. Those two are in paradise living the dream. God has given them everything they need. Sure, there is one tree that he has made off limits, but they have all these other trees, with all of their needs provided.

So, again, what's the problem?

Well..., the snake shows up with his sly mind games. He shifts Eve's focus off all the beautiful fruit trees in the garden that God has given to them to eat "freely" (Genesis 2:16 KJV). Suddenly, she only sees the one tree that they are not allowed to eat from.

Have we ever fallen prey to this same tactic? For instance, our car is working perfectly with no mechanical issues. It serves its purpose and gets us to and from work or wherever we need to go. Then, the neighbor pulls up in a brand-new car with bells and whistles we have never even heard of. Suddenly, our car is not good enough. We only see the car we want. Or our finances seem to be up to par. We are paying all of our bills with enough left over for a few extras here and there. But then we overhear a coworker sharing how much he makes, which happens to be much more than our salary. Are we still satisfied or do we begin to grumble about not making enough money?

Oh, how quickly we can lose sight of the blessings we have and only see what we do not!

In Philippians 4:11-12, Paul wrote, "Not that I speak in respect of want: for I have learned, in whatsoever state I am, therewith to be content. I know both how to be abased, and I know how to abound: every where and in all things I am instructed both to be full and to be hungry, both to abound and to suffer need" (KJV). Note that Paul was in prison when he wrote this letter.

In 1 Thessalonians 5:18, Paul instructs, "In every thing give thanks: for this is the will of God in Christ Jesus concerning you" (KJV). He does not say to give thanks when I feel like it or only when life is grand. He says, "In every thing give thanks...," and he also says, "... this is the will of God...." Giving thanks is a command from God.

The enemy doesn't want us to give thanks to God. He wants to slither in and take our eyes off our blessings. Sometimes, when things are going bad, it's hard not to wallow in our hardship. And on this earth, some face much greater hardships, obstacles, and loss than others. But when we stop and actually name off the things we have to be thankful for... all of those things that we would not want to wake up without tomorrow, we see just how blessed we really are.

BIBLE READING: GENESIS 2; PHILIPPIANS 4:11-12; 1 THESSALONIANS 5:18

A Cry for Help

"I MUST WORK THE WORKS OF HIM THAT SENT ME, WHILE IT IS DAY: THE NIGHT COMETH, WHEN NO MAN CAN WORK."
JOHN 9:4 KJV

My husband and I have been married for almost twenty-six years. Every morning, I still walk him to the door when he leaves, and every evening, I listen for the sound of his truck coming up the drive and meet him at the door. Why? Because I miss him when we aren't together, and I look forward to seeing him when he gets home.

When my children come home, my husband and I listen for them... and what do we do? We run to the door to hug them and greet them.

However, when a stranger comes to the door, even deliveries, I usually do not even go to the door if the bell rings. If it is a package, the driver will leave it at the door, and for safety reasons, I do not open my door for strangers.

In the fifth chapter of Mark, we are told of a man with superhuman strength. He cannot be bound by anything human-made, yet he cries non-stop and hurts himself. *"And when he was come out of the ship, immediately there met him out of the tombs a man with an unclean spirit, Who had his dwelling among the tombs; and no man could bind him, no, not with chains: Because that he had been often bound with fetters and chains, and the chains had been plucked asunder by him, and the fetters broken in pieces: neither could any man tame him. And always, night and day, he was in the mountains, and in the tombs, crying, and cutting himself with stones"* (Mark 5:2-5 KJV). I picture a man being tormented as if he has some sort of slow-eating disease that has him teetering on the edge, clinging to his will to live yet longing desperately to end the pain. And in the midst of this brutal tug-of-war, I note in verse two that the man does not wait for his path to cross with Jesus. Instead, he goes to meet Jesus. It does not say why, but as in my opening example, do we rush to meet someone we do not want to see?

And, I believe that he rushed to meet Jesus because it details in Mark 5:2 that he, "...immediately there met him..." (KJV). To me, this implies a deliberate and diligent act. But why would this man with an unclean spirit want to see Jesus so badly that he would meet Him as soon as He came off the boat? Again, it does not say, but I think this man wants help and knows Jesus can help him.

What does Jesus do? He helps him. We read in Mark 5:8, "For He said unto him, Come out of the man, thou unclean spirit" (KJV).

This man's situation illustrates the grim battle with darkness that we are up against. Yet, the battle and the warning were not the only thoughts swirling in my brain as I pondered this story. As I read this scripture, I could not stop thinking about this man's cry for help. These unclean spirits were controlling this man's body, yet he ran to meet Jesus. This man was in there crying for help. It made me wonder how many people we come in contact with each day who are crying out for help. Not speaking in terms of demon possession, but in terms of those we encounter who may be sad or lonely or have an aching void they are desperate to fill. Do we react as Jesus did?

Do we tell them about Jesus? Do we even stop and take notice, or do we walk on past?

In John 9:4, Jesus says, "I must work the works of him that sent me, while it is day: the night cometh, when no man can work" (KJV).

Let us do God's work now. Let us use the time God has given us to hear those cries for help and proclaim the Good News of our Savior.

BIBLE READING: JOHN 9:4; MARK 5:2-8

Breaking Point

"It is of the Lord's mercies that we are not consumed, because His compassions fail not. They are new every morning: great is thy faithfulness." Lamentations 3:22-23 KJV

She sits at the kitchen table staring at a computer screen, attempting to help her children with homework. *How can they change math?* Shaking her head, she types "new multiplication" into the search engine, trying to find a short video. *And why can't kids have real textbooks anymore?* She keeps glancing at the clock. She had tossed a frozen pizza in the oven ten minutes ago when she ran in the door. Guilt gnaws at her for serving her family frozen pizza for dinner, but after a long day of waiting tables, trying to help the kids with schoolwork, and still laundry and bills to take care of, that is just all she has time for. She knows her husband deserves a better meal. He has had a long day at work too.

"Don't you have any notes on this? Daddy will be home in a few minutes, and we still need to have dinner."

"But Mom...we have to fix my project tonight. It's due tomorrow, and you did it wrong. There are only eight planets. You said there were nine."

"There are nine planets." She sings a little sentence she learned in school to help her remember them.

Her son shakes his head. "That's not how it goes." He starts to sing his version then gets confused. "Just look it up. Pluto is not a planet."

Letting out a sigh, she types 'planets' into the search bar. *What? How can they get rid of a planet?* She gazes at the solar system model in the corner and drops her head.

"Mom...Mom...I smell something burning!"

"Great. Now we don't even have frozen pizza for dinner," she mumbles under her breath as she runs to the kitchen and pulls the blackened cheese from the oven. *I just can't seem to get it right.* A lulling ache settles in her chest. *How did we get so far in debt that we work ourselves to death? No matter how fast I move, I can't seem to get it all done. I can't catch a break. I can't even catch my breath.* She squeezes her eyes shut, trying to push down the tears. *If we hadn't gone into debt for all of this meaningless stuff, we wouldn't have to work all this overtime. But everyone else seems to keep up. Why am I such a failure? I can't even heat a frozen pizza or help my kids multiply two numbers. I am running as fast as I can, and life is still passing me by. I wonder what happened to Pluto.*

Have you ever felt like the woman in my fictional story above? I am not speaking of the details like burning a pizza or messing up homework. I'm talking about running so fast and trying so hard to keep up that exhaustion sets in, the enemy starts whispering, and you feel like you have reached the breaking point. I am going to guess that at one time or another in our lives, we all have. At least, I have.

In 1 Kings 17-19, the Lord tells Elijah to hide by the brook Cherinth which will provide him with water. As Elijah hides by the brook, the ravens bring him food. But after a while, because there is no rain, the brook dries up, and the Lord sends Elijah to Zarephath where a widow gives him food and water. Many days pass and the woman's son becomes ill and dies. Elijah prays over the boy, and he is revived. At the end of the drought, Elijah challenges the prophets of Baal on Mount Carmel where he prays, and fire comes down from Heaven consuming his sacrifice. Jezebel finds out about the fire from Heaven and wants Elijah dead. Elijah runs into the wilderness, collapses beneath a tree, and asks God to let him die. 1 Kings 19:4 details, "But he himself went a day's journey into the wilderness, and came and sat down under a juniper tree: and he requested for himself that he might die; and said, It is enough; now, O Lord, take away my life; for I am not better than my fathers" (KJV).

Now, why did I just summarize this story in a fast-paced and exhaustive manner? Because the details of this story show a man that is exhausted, and inside, he feels like a failure. He has reached his breaking point. He is depressed, and as an escape from his mental torment of depression, he prays for God to end his life. But how does God answer Elijah's request? Well, God doesn't let Elijah die. Instead, he provides for Elijah's real needs. He lets Elijah rest, and then He sends an angel to feed him. He lets Elijah rest some more and then sends an angel to feed him again (1 Kings 19:4-8).

So, what can we learn from this story? Even the great prophet Elijah went through a brief period of depression. But God was not finished with Elijah. Instead, He restored Elijah. He saw his need for rest and renewal, and He provided for that need. So, when we feel overwhelmed, we should take the time to be still and let God renew us because just as God saw and understood Elijah's need, God will understand your need and my need too. AND GOD GIVES US EACH DAY BECAUSE HE HAS A PURPOSE FOR OUR LIVES.

BIBLE READING: 1 KINGS 17-19

He Never Knew the Easy Life

"BUT GODLINESS WITH CONTENTMENT IS GREAT GAIN." 1 TIMOTHY 6:6 KJV

He never knew the easy life. Indulgence and prosperity were only words... words that would never describe his earthly journey, yet he pressed on. My grandfather was born in a small mountain town in 1923. His father died of pneumonia when he was three, and he lost his mother to illness a few years later. Orphaned at the age of seven, he pressed on.

He went to live with his older brother and his wife. And while he had a home in a familiar place with family, times were difficult. He was also a child growing up during the Great Depression when warmth and food were luxuries. Yet, he pressed on. My grandfather often reminisced, telling stories of young men getting paid a quarter to jump on the trains and toss off coal as they came through town so people could have a little heat in their homes. He detailed the excitement of getting a filling meal of possum or carp.

After only completing the sixth grade, he had to leave school to help feed the family. His first job was breaking beans for seventy-five cents a day. Then, as a teen, he worked, cutting timber and other various jobs to help feed the family. When he came of age, he joined the army, serving during World War II. His time overseas was mostly spent in engineering, building airstrips and bridges, but nonetheless, it was dark and grim. He described the image of bullet-pierced helmets scattering the beach when he arrived in Normandy. But he pressed on, and his time in service took him all the way to the Battle of the Bulge.

After returning home to his small mountain town, he married, worked long hours, and obtained a small house. There, he lived on a fixed budget without central heat and air conditioning or a washer or dryer until he passed at the age of 88.

He never complained. Instead, he pressed on.

In his letter to the Philippians, Paul writes from prison, "Not that I speak in respect of want: for I have learned, in whatsoever state I am, therewith to be content. I know both how to be abased, and I know how to abound: every where and in all things I am instructed both to be full and to be hungry, both to abound and to suffer need" (Philippians 4:11-12 KJV).

My grandfather is a prime example of these words. Whatever this life threw at him, he chose to press on. He sacrificed his education and his childhood to provide for his family. He sacrificed his time, risking his life in war for our freedom. He chose to press on, and he chose to be content in doing it. As a child, I spent countless hours with him while my parents worked. We played games and went to the grocery store and the laundromat. I watched him tend to his tomato garden and make birdhouses out of hollow gourds. But, what I remember most is how he found happiness wherever he was and in whatever he had.

Let us be filled with the joy and contentment that comes from the Father... the joy that keeps us pressing on despite our circumstances and the contentment that Paul speaks of in his letter.

BIBLE READING: 1 TIMOTHY 6:6; PHILIPPIANS 4:11-12

When the Enemy Attacks

"THERE HATH NO TEMPTATION TAKEN YOU BUT SUCH AS IS COMMON TO MAN: BUT GOD IS FAITHFUL, WHO WILL NOT SUFFER YOU TO BE TEMPTED ABOVE THAT YE ARE ABLE; BUT WILL WITH THE TEMPTATION ALSO MAKE A WAY TO ESCAPE, THAT YE MAY BE ABLE TO BEAR IT." 1 CORINTHIANS 10:13 KJV

He lurks in the shadows waiting for the perfect moment. He watches. He listens. His narrow gaze fixes on her as she stares at the phone. A single tear trickles down her cheek.

Now, he tells himself. He whisks from the darkness just long enough to let a whisper penetrate her thoughts. *"No one cares."* In a blink, he slithers back to the shadows, knowing he made progress.

She lowers her head with those words repeating in her mind. *No one cares. No one cares.* Her body trembles as she sobs into her hands.

He holds his head high as he watches her cry. Tomorrow he will cut a little deeper. Soon, he will have her believing that she truly is all alone.

Although the above is a fictional account, this scenario depicts how the enemy works. Just as the young lady in the story is feeling lonely and the enemy swoops in and preys on her fragile state, the devil watches and waits for a moment of weakness in our lives, so he can whisper a lie that will paralyze us or veer us from the TRUTH.

Now, here is a humorous illustration that involves our dog, but let me point out that our dog is a gift and a blessing to our family from God. As a matter of fact, her middle name is "Angel," and in no way am I comparing our dog to the enemy. I am merely pointing out our dog's ability to utilize my daughter's weakness to fill her stomach. You see, our dog has special treats that she is only supposed to get when my husband and I have our cup of coffee before bed. However, our precious dog is clever. She is aware that as long as my husband and I are present, no exceptions will occur. On the contrary, our dog is in tune to the fact that my daughter cannot stand to hear her cry. So, guess what? If the dog gets my daughter alone, the saddest doggy face appears along with nonstop whimpering until my daughter's soft heart cannot stand it anymore, and the master of the "appeal to pity" fallacy has an extra treat for the day.

So, how do we protect ourselves from an enemy that knows and attacks our weaknesses? First, we need to recognize what our weaknesses are. For example, my weakness is my OCD, and the enemy loves to plant those "what if" thoughts in my mind that paralyze me with worry. Being aware of this does not make the battle easy, but I know I need extra armor in that area. And second, since I just mentioned armor, we need to put on our spiritual armor daily. We need to surround ourselves with TRUTH, cover our hearts with righteousness, plant our feet firmly in our faith, guard our minds through our salvation, keep our shield up to extinguish the arrows, and have the sword ready to use offensively and defensively (see Ephesians 6:13-17). In Matthew 4, each time Jesus was tempted, he quoted scripture by saying, "It is written..." (Matthew 4:4,

4:7, 4:10 KJV). So, we need to study scripture in order to keep our swords sharpened.

In 1 Corinthians 10:13, we are assured, "There hath no temptation taken you but such as is common to man: but God is faithful, who will not suffer you to be tempted above that ye are able; but will with the temptation also make a way to escape, that ye may be able to bear it" (KJV). God had given us the spiritual armor we need..., but we have to apply it... put on each piece... daily.

BIBLE READING: MATTHEW 4; EPHESIANS 6:13-17; 1 CORINTHIANS 10:13

Surrounded

> "IN GOD HAVE I PUT MY TRUST: I WILL NOT
> BE AFRAID WHAT MAN CAN DO UNTO ME."
> PSALM 56:11 KJV

Surrounded... yet he did not cower. His enemies tried to debate, but their rebuttal held no ground against his words of truth. He knew God's Word and he spoke without hesitation. So, they spread lies until they had stirred an angry mob against Stephen. And still, as he stood surrounded by people who wanted him to die, Stephen did not betray his Savior, nor did one word escape his lips that he would ever be ashamed of. Instead, Stephen spoke TRUTH.

They heard Stephen, and they knew. The Bible says, "When they heard these things, they were cut to the heart..." (Acts 7:54 KJV). But these men rejected the light and sunk deeper into darkness, for the same verse of scripture goes on, illustrating their next action by detailing, "...and they gnashed on him with their teeth" (Acts 7:54 KJV).

Hmmm. That phrase sounds familiar. In Matthew 13:50, Jesus used similar wording in his description of the end times when the wicked are thrown into the fire. He says, "...there shall be wailing and gnashing of teeth" (Matthew 13:50 KJV).

From the use of that phrase, I conclude that Stephen was surrounded by a much greater darkness than a few men who desired to stir an argument. Stephen was surrounded by forces of darkness that were fueled by hate. Stephen's words of TRUTH hit home. These men knew he spoke TRUTH, and it enraged them.

Stephen could have elected to back down. He could have chosen to deliver a different speech to appease his audience. He could have blended with his earthly surroundings. But he did not.

Paul states in Philippians 1:21, "For me to live is Christ, and to die is gain" (KJV). And in Psalm 56:11, David proclaims, "In God have I put my trust: I will not be afraid what man can do unto me" (KJV).

Yes, evil men chose to end Stephen's earthly life... but his Savior was waiting.

"But he, being full of the Holy Ghost, looked up stedfastly into heaven, and saw the glory of God, and Jesus standing on the right hand of God, And said, Behold, I see the heavens opened, and the Son of man standing on the right hand of God." Acts 7:55-56 KJV

When I think back to watching my children play sports or perform in various activities, as a proud parent, my instinctive reaction to a job well done was to leap to my feet and cheer. It did not matter if anyone else clapped or stood, if my child did something great, my husband and I would give them a standing ovation.

I believe that is why Stephen saw Jesus standing. Jesus was so proud of Stephen's faith and character. At the end of Stephen's speech, Jesus leaped to his feet, welcoming Stephen to his eternal home with a standing ovation.

Imagine that... entering Heaven with a standing ovation by Jesus.

BIBLE READING: ACTS 7; PSALM 56:11; MATTHEW 13:50; PHILIPPIANS 1:21

It's In the Perspective

"FOR MY THOUGHTS ARE NOT YOUR THOUGHTS, NEITHER ARE YOUR WAYS MY WAYS, SAITH THE LORD. FOR AS THE HEAVENS ARE HIGHER THAN THE EARTH, SO ARE MY WAYS HIGHER THAN YOUR WAYS, AND MY THOUGHTS THAN YOUR THOUGHTS." ISAIAH 55:8-9 KJV

My father was classified as color blind. When I was a child, he showed me images made of dots of various sizes and colors that were supposed to test for color blindness. A person who was color blind would not see the same image as one who did not have the impairment. One, in particular, that I recall had a teapot and a teacup. I could clearly see the smaller coffee mug and the larger teapot, whereas my dad could only see the coffee mug.

In our world, life often seems unfair. Some struggle financially their entire lives while others are born into riches, wasting more than others will ever have. Some are athletic, while some (like me) can trip over their own feet just walking across the room. If we look at fairness through the eyes of the world, this list of comparisons could be endless. And the enemy has a knack for pinpointing that one thing we feel is unfair and taunting us with it... just as he did in the beginning with Eve. He managed to put her focus on the one tree that she was not supposed to eat of while blinding her to the bountiful blessings surrounding her (See Genesis 3:1-5 KJV). And, when God asked Moses to go to the Pharoah, Moses' first thoughts were not on his positive attributes or the reason God was selecting him for this task, but rather on what he saw as a weakness: his speech (See Exodus 4:10 KJV).

In the Old Testament, Jeremiah was a great prophet sent by God to deliver a message. Yet, just as being a Christian does not make us exempt from trials and tribulations or the devil's constant stumbling blocks, his devotion and obedience to God did not make him exempt from the suffering, persecution, or his own human emotion brought upon by the ways of the world.

Here are a few key points that spoke to me as I have studied this section of scripture.

First, I noted that in Jeremiah 12:1-2, he questions the prosperity of those who did not truly follow God. As I read these verses, I could vividly visualize this faithful man called by God to deliver a message but still battling his own human thoughts in the process. I could imagine this little whisper repeating... *it's not fair... it's not fair.* Jeremiah questions in a respectful manner, "Righteous art thou, O Lord, when I plead with thee: yet let me talk with thee of thy judgments: Wherefore doth the way of the wicked prosper? wherefore are all they happy that deal very treacherously? Thou hast planted them, yea, they have taken root: they grow, yea, they bring forth fruit: thou art near in their mouth, and far from their reins" (Jeremiah 12:1-2 KJV). Of course, Jeremiah knows the truth. After all, he has been sent on this mission to warn them of their demise because of their actions. Yet, for a moment, he still has to battle his human thinking... those thoughts the enemy tosses to throw us off.

Second, he was not exempt from depression and sadness. In Chapter 15, he even questions his own existence, wondering if it would not have been better if he had never been born. He laments, "Woe is me, my mother, that thou hast borne me a man of strife and a man of contention to the whole earth! I have neither lent on usury, nor men have lent to me on usury; yet every one of them doth curse me" (Jeremiah 15:10 KJV). Of course, the truth is that God had great purpose for Jeremiah. God had created him to deliver a message. But even so, Jeremiah still struggled with some of the very thoughts that plague so many today.

Third, God tells Jeremiah not to marry or have children. "Thou shalt not take thee a wife, neither shalt thou have sons or daughters in this place" (Jeremiah 16:2 KJV). When I got to this verse, I stopped and thought of the many times that God may tell us, "No," or not answer a prayer the way we want. But as I continued to read, I understood that God was sparing Jeremiah more pain. Jeremiah 16:3-4 details, "For thus saith the Lord concerning the sons and concerning the daughters that are born in this place, and concerning their mothers that bare them, and concerning their fathers that begat them in this land; They shall die of grievous deaths..."(KJV). These verses remind me that God knows tomorrow, and his answers to our prayers do not always align with our present wants, but rather with what He knows is best for our future.

Sometimes we may question our pain, our tribulations, and unanswered prayers. But just as my dad could only see the small teacup, we cannot see the whole picture. While Eve saw a rule she did not understand, God knew eating from that one tree would have serious consequences. While Moses saw his own weakness, God knew what he had created him to do. While Jeremiah was currently suffering and witnessing those around him prosper, God knew what was coming for those who were disobeying him. And even though Jeremiah probably wanted a family, God knew the pain he would endure as the people around him were killed in the invasion.

While we see only a small frame, God views the entire movie at once. We have no idea what the next minute holds, but God has already seen tomorrow. And in Isaiah 55:8-9, we are told, "For my thoughts are not your thoughts, neither are your ways my ways, saith the Lord. For as the Heavens are higher than the earth, so are my ways higher than your ways, and my thoughts than your thoughts". (KJV).

BIBLE READING: JEREMIAH 12,15, 16:2-4; ISAIAH 55:8-9

Discerning the Truth

"STUDY TO SHEW THYSELF APPROVED UNTO GOD, A WORKMAN THAT NEEDETH NOT TO BE ASHAMED, RIGHTLY DIVIDING THE WORD OF TRUTH." 2 TIMOTHY 2:15 KJV

A while back, I was assembling a wall cabinet for my daughter's bathroom. I was in a bit of a hurry, so instead of reading the directions verbatim, I sort of skimmed and looked at the pictures. When I finished, it looked great... until I picked it up, and the bottom panel almost fell off. In my rushed skimming process, I skipped over one important sentence which instructed me to insert two screws into the bottom panel. *Hmmm... I suppose that would have explained the leftover hardware.*

The shelf I had assembled was not sturdy or strong enough to hang on the wall because I had not thoroughly read the instructions. In the same way, my knowledge of God's Word will not be strong or reliable if I do not read it daily and in context, which allows the enemy a window of opportunity to swoop in and deceive me. After all, Satan even used scripture out of context to tempt Jesus in the wilderness. In Matthew 4:6, Satan refers to Psalm 91:11-12 when he says to Jesus, "...If thou be the Son of God, cast thyself down: for it is written, He shall give his angels charge concerning thee: and in their hands they shall bear thee up, lest at any time thou dash thy foot against a stone" (KJV). But knowing the scripture, in the next verse, Jesus quickly responded with words from Deuteronomy 6:16, "...It is written again, Thou shalt not tempt the Lord thy God" (Matthew 4:7 KJV).

Paul warns of the enemy's tactics in 2 Corinthians 11:14-15 as he explains, "And no marvel; for Satan himself is transformed into an angel of light. Therefore it is no great thing if his ministers also be transformed as the ministers of righteousness; whose end shall be according to their works" (KJV). Just as the enemy tried to appear knowledgeable of God's Word, twisting the meaning to fit his needs and tempt Jesus, he will also try to fool us, hence, proving the importance of reading and absorbing God's Word daily ... really absorbing its TRUTH in its entirety, so we will not be deceived by the enemy in disguise.

Through the years, my children have had quite a few books to read for school, usually followed by a test. If my children had only read the summary of a book or had depended on someone else to tell them what the book was about, they would not have done well. They would have missed important details that could only be known by reading the entire book themselves.

In the same way, if we do not read the Bible for ourselves, we may miss important details... details that we could use to defend against Satan's lies.

Remember that the Word of God is an offensive and defensive weapon. If we know the TRUTH, we are already on the offense, and then when the enemy comes lurking, we can defend ourselves against those lies.

BIBLE READING: 2 TIMOTHY 2:15; 2 CORINTHIANS 11:14-15; MATTHEW 4

This is the Day

"THIS IS THE DAY WHICH THE LORD HATH MADE; WE WILL REJOICE AND BE GLAD IN IT." PSALM 118:24 KJV

I open my eyes and jump to my feet. The snooze button is not an option. Time does not allow it. As I fell asleep last night, I made a plan of all the things I wanted to accomplish today. I trudge down the stairs going over the list in my mind and then dive right in. Devotion time, prayer time, workout, clean kitchen, get dressed, check email, and then I am off to run errands. I take off the trash, stop by the college bookstore to pick up textbooks for my son, and while I am out, I stop by the store for a few things I need. Thinking about the book trailer I am working on and the basket I need to make for the book signing, I move at my normal fast pace through the store.

And as usual, I find myself delayed at the bananas because even the green ones have a brown tint. While I stand there, staring at the bananas, trying to decide on a bunch that might remain edible for a couple of days, I begin to talk to the lady next to me about how cold it is in the store, and she comments about how she wishes she had brought a jacket. Then she proceeds to ask me if I know Jesus. Suddenly, the urgent list vanishes from my mind. I answer, "Yes," and the lady and I talk for a few minutes about how wonderful it is to walk with Jesus every day, and the need to tell others about Him. After a bit of sharing, I continue with my shopping but in a renewed frame of mind. My brain is no longer whirling with items not checked off on my list or what I will be doing three hours from now. My thoughts are no longer weighed down with worry about not meeting my goals. Instead, I am thinking about how I should be opening my eyes and taking in the people around me. Am I walking right past someone with whom I should be sharing the Gospel? Is there someone right next to me who needs to hear about Jesus?

After my epiphany that day at the store and the realization of how the enemy can start distracting me the second I open my eyes, I began working on my issue of setting unrealistic goals for the day. And, I made a change to the way I pray in the morning. In the past, I would often find myself praying for God to help me focus and get everything completed that I needed to. Now each morning, I pray that God will help me accomplish what He has planned for me to do that day. However, I am a planner, and letting go of my planned list is a struggle. So, I ask God to help me move my eyes from my list to His list. That said, I am certain my brief meeting at the banana stand was not by chance. I needed an eye-opener to remind me of my purpose and shift my perspective to the correct to-do list. After all, each day is a gift from God. And that was the verse that continued to repeat in my head that day. "This is the day which the Lord hath made; we will rejoice and be glad in it" (Psalm 118:24 KJV).

If God made the day, then the day belongs to Him, not me. And two words in the above verse catch my attention... "rejoice" and "glad."

BIBLE READING: PSALM 118:24

The Richest Man

"FOR WHERE YOUR TREASURE IS, THERE WILL YOUR HEART BE ALSO." MATTHEW 6:21 KJV

L et me tell you about the richest man I have ever met.

***

Tears streak faces all around the room. Hugs and stories pass between friends and family. Children and grandchildren write heartfelt notes and tuck them in his pocket. Some of the older grandchildren are dressed in his flannel shirts as they long to hold on to him and keep him close. As family and friends gather here to remember and honor this life, my eyes are opened to the person I aspire to be. So many memories flood through my mind that I will never forget like how he loved to make people laugh with his jokes, how he would only eat his food if it was a little on the burnt side, *...and the time I got mad because he put paper in my straw when we went out to eat...and the sound of his voice singing "Happy Birthday" to me over the phone every year ...and how he would aggravate me about drinking all of his coffee....* But it was his devotion to God that is etched in my mind and will forever be close to my heart.

He did not just accept the gift of salvation. He lived to serve God. He knew the Bible front to back, and I have been told that he would study God's Word for hours on end. The appearance of his Bible shouts this man's love for God and his longing to have a close and personal relationship with his Heavenly Father. His thumb and fingerprints are permanently indented on the cover from holding it when he preached. The tattered pages from years and years of use are filled with his handwritten notes. Apparently, he purchased the Bible just a few weeks after accepting Christ, and his excitement and joy are evident because on the dedication page next to 'Occasion,' he wrote, "Celebrating finding God." *He was celebrating!*

From the looks of this Bible now, he never stopped celebrating because it is obvious it was opened and used daily. If someone asked a question about his faith, he would not answer without opening his Bible and pointing out the scriptures. When God called him to preach, he never accepted money. He did not want to be paid to share his love for God. He just wanted to spread the Gospel. This man impacted so many lives from the Americans he sacrificed for in the Korean War, to the lonely elderly lady whom his church group brought and shared Thanksgiving dinner with, to the hungry stranger who he bought a hamburger for, to the family and friends in this chapel mourning our loss. Take note that I use the words "our loss" because Paul said in Philippians 1:21, "For to me to live is Christ, and to die is gain" (KJV). There is no doubt that as this man entered into the kingdom of Heaven, he heard his Father proclaim the words, "...Well done, good and faithful servant..." (Matthew 25:23 KJV). He let God shine through his life, and even in his last breath on earth, God used this faithful servant to reveal His mighty presence.

In our society, the word rich usually relates to having assets and a lot of money. In Matthew 6:20-21, Jesus instructs us to, "...lay up for yourselves treasures in heaven, where neither moth nor rust doth corrupt, and where thieves do not break through nor steal: For where your treasure is, there will your heart be also" (KJV). This man stored up his treasure where it mattered and bequeathed a legacy of faith to all who knew him. The tears, the sincere sentiments in the handwritten notes, and the teens in flannel are priceless acts of love for a man who left a permanent impression on every life he touched. I feel so blessed to have had the honor of calling this man "Dad" and even more blessed that he treated me as his daughter. This great man is my father-in-law, but to me, he is "Dad." And, he is the kind of person I want to be.

I do not want to just get into Heaven. I want to follow the example of this man I call "Dad" and make my life count for God.

So today, where are we storing our treasures? Are we bequeathing our children a house that will crumble or a firm foundation built on Christ?

When we see Jesus face to face, let's be faithful with the blessings and the work He has given us, and let us long to hear our Heavenly Father say, "...Well done, good and faithful servant; thou hast been faithful over a few things, I will make thee ruler over many things: enter thou into the joy of the Lord" (Matthew 25:23 KJV).

BIBLE READING: MATTHEW 6:19-21; PHILIPPIANS 1:21; MATTHEW 25:23

The Good Soil

"BUT HE THAT RECEIVED SEED INTO THE GOOD GROUND IS HE THAT HEARETH THE WORD, AND UNDERSTANDETH IT; WHICH ALSO BEARETH FRUIT, AND BRINGETH FORTH, SOME AN HUNDREDFOLD, SOME SIXTY, SOME THIRTY." MATTHEW 13:23 KJV

Jesus often told parables to help the people better understand his message, and in Matthew 13, he relates the story of the sower and the seed. As I read this parable the other day, I could not help but reflect on some of my own gardening skills as I pondered each scenario.

The first example is given in Matthew 13:4. "And when he sowed, some seeds fell by the way side, and the fowls came and devoured them up" (KJV). In other words, the seed fell on hard ground. Since the soil was not soft or tilled, the seed just laid right there on top.

Picture it... it has not rained in weeks. The yard is covered in bare spots, so I decide to toss out some grass seed. But I do not do anything to prepare the ground. Instead, I scatter a few handfuls of seed and go back inside, thinking nature will run its course. A while later, I look out the window and witness nature taking its course because the yard is filled with happy birds devouring the feast that I have provided.

Jesus goes on to explain the meaning in Matthew 13:19. "When any one heareth the word of the kingdom, and understandeth it not, then cometh the wicked one, and catcheth away that which was sown in his heart. This is he which received seed by the way side" (KJV). The Word of God is heard, but not absorbed or understood. The heart is hard and untouched, so the devil quickly snatches it from any line of thought... *like the birds that ate my grass seed.*

The second example comes in Matthew 13:5-6. "Some fell upon stony places, where they had not much earth: and forthwith they sprung up, because they had no deepness of earth: And when the sun was up, they were scorched; and because they had no root, they withered away" (KJV).

My mishap does not involve stones, but nonetheless, it is the image that came to me as I read these verses:

When my husband and I moved into our first house, I thought it would be pretty to have hanging baskets on our front porch. So, we purchased four ferns. I had good intentions. I watered them (almost) every day. But every time I watered them, the water immediately drained out through the holes in the bottom of the pots. After a couple of days, the ends of the leaves started to turn brown, and not too many days later, (I might have actually forgotten to water them that day), I came home to find no survivors. All four were withered and scorched from the hot sun.

In verses 20 and 21 of Matthew, chapter thirteen, Jesus explains, "But he that received the seed into stony places, the same is he that heareth the word, and anon with joy receiveth it; Yet hath he not root in himself, but dureth for a while: for when tribulation or persecution ariseth because of the word, by and by he is offended" (KJV). My ferns looked good for a few days, but because the pot was not holding water, and the roots had no means in a hanging basket to extend those roots deep in the ground to reach the hydration they needed, they could not handle the heat. In the same way, some hear the Word of God and accept it for a bit, but when trouble arises and tribulation strikes, they cannot handle the heat and abandon their faith.

The third example appears in Matthew 13:7. "And some fell among thorns; and the thorns sprung up, and choked them" (KJV).

When I look at my landscaping, I often wonder why weeds are so easy to grow. They need no attention at all, and they multiply faster than one can use a calculator. Yet, if I blink, the shrubs and flowers that I want to grow are overtaken by the weeds and sometimes get to the point that I cannot decipher which is the plant and which is the weed.

Jesus interprets this example in Matthew 13:22. "He also that received seed among the thorns is he that heareth the word; and the care of this world, and the deceitfulness of riches, choke the word, and he becometh unfruitful" (KJV). Just as the plants in my landscaping get lost among the weeds, a person can hear the Word of God and accept it but have so many other priorities that they never grow or produce any spiritual fruit. The Word becomes buried beneath their worldly desires.

The final example is given in Matthew 13:8. "But other fell into good ground, and brought forth fruit, some an hundredfold, some sixtyfold, some thirtyfold" (KJV).

These would be the plants at my mother's house. She has a natural green thumb... a trait that was not passed on to me. My mother has always loved plants... and her house is infiltrated with them, inside and out. Of course, different types of plants have different needs and require different environments. My mother has studied and developed a wealth of knowledge on how to care for each one.

In Matthew 13:23, Jesus describes the seed in the good soil. "But he that received seed into the good ground is he that heareth the word, and understandeth it; which also beareth fruit, and bringeth forth, some an hundredfold, some sixty, some thirty" (KJV).

Just as desirable plants are not going to flourish if they are not tended to, our faith is not going to grow if we neglect to nurture it. If we want to grow in our walk with Christ and bear spiritual fruit, we need to spend time reading our Bible, absorbing as much of God's Word as we possibly can, and we need to spend time with our Heavenly Father, making our relationship with Him our FIRST PRIORITY.

BIBLE READING: MATTHEW 13

Hopeless? Never!

"FOR WITH GOD NOTHING SHALL BE IMPOSSIBLE." LUKE 1:37 KJV

I love to go to the beach and stare at the ocean, absorbing its beauty and magnitude. However, I do not care much for swimming in it. I can swim, but I am not a confident swimmer. The ocean has too many unknowns such as that ginormous wave that seems to pop up when you least expect it and that sudden strong undertow that wants to pull you out to sea just after that ginormous wave has just knocked you to the sandy ocean bottom. That being said, I prefer to admire the mighty splendor of the ocean and enjoy the peaceful lullaby of the breaking waves from a beach chair situated a safe distance from the water.

Sometimes, well maybe more often than sometimes, life is like my description of swimming in the ocean. A wave knocks you down and before you can get your footing, some other obstacle sneaks up and drags you further off course. That's when the enemy swoops in and tries to convince us that our situation is hopeless.

In Exodus, chapter 14, the children of Israel were being pursued by the Egyptian army. I'm sure they thought their situation was hopeless and were certain they were going to die.

"And when Pharaoh drew nigh, the children of Israel lifted up their eyes, and, behold, the Egyptians marched after them; and they were sore afraid: and the children of Israel cried out unto the Lord. And they said unto Moses, Because there were no graves in Egypt, hast thou taken us away to die in the wilderness? wherefore hast thou dealt thus with us, to carry us forth out of Egypt?" Exodus 14:10-11 KJV.

But, as we know, God parted the Red Sea, and the children of Israel passed through the water on dry land. Can you imagine what it must have looked like? A humongous wall of water is standing at attention on both sides, appearing as if it could collapse on top of you at any moment. Of course, that is what happened to their pursuers. (See Exodus 14:22-23 KJV).

Two points stand out to me as I ponder this story. First, with God, no situation is ever hopeless because nothing is impossible with God. The children of Israel were trapped between an approaching army and a huge body of water. It seemed there was no way out. But...

- *"For with God nothing shall be impossible." Luke 1:37 KJV.*

The problem did not disappear. Instead, God made a way through the problem.

And two, sometimes God's answer to our problem requires us to take a step of faith.

- *"Trust in the Lord with all thine heart; and lean not unto thine own understanding." Proverbs 3:5 KJV*

Even with an army chasing them, that first step between those giant walls of water was probably a bit tough. (I imagine walking between two waves the size of tsunamis.) But since we do not know what tomorrow holds, our hope lies with the One who does. Faith requires action. We must step out in faith and trust Him completely.

BIBLE READING: EXODUS 14; LUKE 1:37; PROVERBS 3:5

One Step at a Time

"THEREFORE WE OUGHT TO GIVE THE MORE EARNEST HEED TO THE THINGS WHICH WE HAVE HEARD, LEST AT ANY TIME WE SHOULD LET THEM SLIP." HEBREWS 2:1 KJV

Standing at the edge of the yard, she stares into the surrounding darkness and then looks over her shoulder at her home enveloped in a yellow aura so bright, it is almost blinding. A feeling of security radiates from the combination of the glow through the windows, the porch light, and the spotlights in the landscaping shining on the house. Outside the well-lit perimeter of the yard is nothing but woods, dense and dark.

Laughter penetrates her ears, and she turns her attention to the thick trees. The sound seems to be coming from just inside the tree line. *One step won't hurt. I just want to see who is there.* She takes a step to the edge of the trees, squinting her eyes, trying to catch sight of someone in the darkness. Nothing but the sound of laughter. *Just another step... or two.* The darkness thickens as the trees begin to block the light from the house. A bit of fear creeps in... but the laughing is getting louder.

The young woman's curiosity trumps her fear, and she presses on a little farther. *What is that?* Now music blends with the laughter. "Hello... hello... is anyone there?" she shouts.

No one replies, but the volume of the music and laughter seem even closer. A few steps deeper, and she calls out again, "HELLO! Who is there?"

When no one responds, chills shoot down her spine. *What was I thinking coming in here? I meant only to step to the edge.* But the music and the laughter pull at her like gravity. *It must be a party. One more step. I could use some fun.*

She takes two more steps, and the laughter turns to shrill screams. She raises her voice, attempting to be heard above the blaring music, but her voice falls on deaf ears. Reality slices through her heart, and she wraps her arms tightly around herself. She is alone... all alone in the darkness. *How did I get here? Why didn't I just go into the house?*

She twists her head, searching frantically for a glimmer of the light. Far off in the distance, a speck glitters. She takes off running as fast as she can, her legs trembling with every stride. The light grows brighter, and the panic echoes from her mouth. "Father, Father, help!"

As she darts from the shroud of the trees, her father leaps from the porch with his arms wide open. She falls into his embrace, and through her quaking sobs, she whimpers, "I'm sorry, Daddy. I should never have left the light."

Her father squeezes her in a hug. "Come inside, my child. Let's sit down and eat."

I have a fear of swimming in the ocean because of the unpredictable activity of the waves. I have often heard how easy it is to be pulled farther from shore than was intended. The same can happen in our relationship with the Father. One morning we are running late and miss our Bible study. Then suddenly we discover we could use that extra ten minutes of sleep, so we decide we will do it before bed. But at night, we fall asleep on the couch, exhausted from the day. Before we know it, we haven't read our Bible or had prayer time in a month. Or perhaps a friend invites us to go somewhere we shouldn't... just this one time... and then we find ourselves in that place day after day... wondering how we got there.

In Hebrews 2:1, we are warned, "Therefore we ought to give the more earnest heed to the things which we have heard, lest at any time we should let them slip" (KJV). We must make a conscious effort to prioritize our relationship with God. Let's not allow ourselves a chance to slip or sink. Let's keep ourselves in His presence.

But, if somehow, we wake up, realizing we have drifted, whether it is a step or a mile, we need to run home... fast. We need to cry out as Peter did when he stepped upon the water and began to sink. In Matthew 14:30-31, we are told, "...he (Peter) was afraid; and beginning to sink, he cried, saying, Lord, save me. And immediately Jesus stretched forth His hand, and caught him..." (KJV).

As in the story of the prodigal son, when the boy realized what he had done and wanted to come home, "...his father saw him, and had compassion, and ran, and fell on his neck, and kissed him" (Luke 15:20 KJV).

Bible Reading: Hebrews 2:1; Matthew 14:30-31; Luke 15:20

What's on the Menu?

"But he answered and said, It is written, Man shall not live by bread alone, but by every word that proceedeth out of the mouth of God." Matthew 4:4 KJV

When I was younger, I had an enormous sweet tooth. Cake, doughnuts, cookies... if it had sugar, I could and would devour it. Every night before bed, I had some sort of dessert, and my favorite and usual treat was a milkshake. It started as a small one, but as time progressed, my cup got larger and larger until my nighttime snack had grown into a 32-ounce peanut butter shake.

However, about ten years ago, my husband and I began a healthy regimen and changed our eating habits. Strangely, if I indulge in something sweet or fried now, it does not set very well. Lethargy sets in, and it feels like I have eaten a brick that refuses to digest. For example, as much as I love the taste of biscuits and gravy, it is one of those meals that makes me want to go back to bed. I would rather begin my day with a bowl of oatmeal or a protein and fruit smoothie that gives me the energy and stamina for an active day. In essence, the food choices that I make affect the overall productivity and outcome of my day.

But our physical bodies are not the only nourishment we need on a daily basis. In Matthew 4:4, when Jesus is being tempted by the devil, He responds by quoting scripture. Jesus answered, "…It is written, Man shall not live by bread alone, but by every word that proceedeth out of the mouth of God" (KJV).

On my journey, I continue to discover the truth in these words more and more. Typically, I read a devotion, study my Bible, recite scripture, and have prayer time first thing each morning. Spending time with God as soon as I get up sets my tone for the day. Reading and quoting verses aloud allows me to not only see God's Word but also audibly hear His word. I begin with my focus on Jesus and fuel my mind and heart with His words, which give me the strength to endure the trials and tribulations in the hours to come.

Yet, the other morning, one little thing after another crept in and disheveled my usual routine. From waking up later than normal to a family member with a sore throat to an early morning appointment, I let my morning Bible study slip through the cracks, and my time with God was rushed. My thoughts were a blur, and I was filled with anxiety. That is not to say that I am anxiety-free on other days. Anxiety is one of my weaknesses and an area that the enemy relentlessly attacks. But on this particular day, I skipped my spiritual breakfast, which affected my ability to extinguish those arrows.

So, let's never miss breakfast with Jesus.

BIBLE READING: MATTHEW 4:4

Our Only Shelter

"I WILL BOTH LAY ME DOWN IN PEACE, AND SLEEP: FOR THOU, LORD, ONLY MAKEST ME DWELL IN SAFETY." PSALM 4:8 KJV

*I*t was an eye-opener, to say the least. I am not one to watch the news regularly nor do I keep a close check on the weather report. I had glimpsed at the news titles of the hurricane that was on track to make landfall in Florida and had heard that our area was expected to get a lot of rain from it. I had also received text alerts as to the preparations being made in the event of a power outage. Yet, I didn't think much about it. I just made a pot of coffee the night before just in case the power was out for a few hours in the morning. When I went to bed Thursday night, the storm was far from my mind, yet anxiety pulsed through me. I told my husband that I was afraid for some reason... that something just did not feel right.

The next morning, I got up as usual, read my devotion, and did my early workout. The storm began to brew and the power flickered, finally giving out a couple of minutes before my husband left for work. The wind gained strength, and a tree fell barely missing the corner of our house. An hour had passed since my husband had gone, and I called to check on him. He was still trying to get to work. I rushed from window to window, listening to the crack of trees uprooting and watching them crash to the ground all around the house. This was the first time I ever remember being truly frightened in a storm.

Two hours passed, and suddenly I couldn't get through on my husband's phone. My heart was pounding, unsure what to do. Then I saw him through the window, walking toward the house. He said he had to leave his truck and trek through the woods. All routes home were blocked by fallen trees and powerlines.

My area was not the hardest hit, yet many in our power district were without electricity for almost two weeks. We were without power four days, and since we have a well, we were without running water also. Yet, this was just a simple inconvenience that does not come anywhere even remotely close to the catastrophic effects that others have endured and are enduring. So many suffered and are still suffering loss. Many lost their homes and jobs. But worst of all, lives were taken by the storm, and many were missing in the aftermath. I cannot even fathom that level of pain and heartbreak.

As I drove down the road and saw the damage left behind and listened to the soul-piercing stories of what some had suffered, the temporary status of this world resonated to my core. Ironically, several days before the storm, I was having trouble sleeping, and my dearest friend texted me a verse to say as a prayer before bed. At the time, I would never have imagined the impact this verse would have had. But after the storm, the words echoed through my mind all day because this world offers no guarantees. True peace and our only real shelter are found in the salvation that comes through a relationship with Jesus. If disaster strikes in the next minute, are we certain of our eternal destination? Can we pray the words in Psalm 4:8 which says, "I will both lay me down in peace, and sleep: for thou, Lord, only makest me dwell in safety" (KJV), knowing that upon our exit from this life, we will enter into His presence?

BIBLE READING: PSALM 4:8

It's Beyond Me

"AND SEEKEST THOU GREAT THINGS FOR THYSELF? SEEK THEM NOT...." JEREMIAH 45:5 KJV

After the three novels were completed and published in my Christian fiction thriller series, I found myself in a new phase of my life. I never expected the empty nest to hit me so hard. Yet, I suppose that after being a stay-at-home mother for twenty-one years, I should have expected to have some emotional confusion. I began doing a lot of soul-searching, praying, and seeking God's guidance for the next phases of my writing career. I needed to hit the pause button so to speak and dig deeper into God's Word. I'm not sure why, but I opened my Bible and immediately chose to study the book of Jeremiah. But as God is in control and I was praying for guidance, I know flipping to that scripture was not a coincidence for this study has touched my heart and given me much to ponder, including the message in the short chapter forty-five.

In this short chapter, the story jumps a little back in time, correlating with the events happening in chapter thirty-six when Jeremiah had Baruch the son of Neriah write down the words God had given. In this latter chapter, we are given a brief glimpse into a moment where Baruch is consumed by self-pity. In Jeremiah 45:3, Baruch is quoted as saying, "...Woe is me now! for the Lord has added grief to my sorrow; I fainted in my sighing, and I find no rest" (KJV).

In reading this chapter, it might be tempting to stand on the outside and focus only on this man's concern for his own comfort and rest, but if I take a step to the inside, I have to ask myself how often I grumble when hardship rains down and the stress level rises. How often in my new phase have I had a moment where I felt like saying, "WOE IS ME"?

So... how does God respond to Baruch's self-pity? In Jeremiah 45:5, He asks Baruch, "And seekest thou great things for thyself?..." (KJV).

I find the question at hand to be rather humbling. As I look at our world and the constant desire to climb to the next level (more money, a bigger house, a better job), this question puts it all in perspective. We are not here for personal fame and fortune. We are not here for the world to see us. We are here for the world to see HIM.

God continues in verse five, instructing Baruch not to seek his own desires and selfish wants, and as the destruction and punishment consume the evil around him, God reminds Baruch that He will protect him wherever he goes. The remainder of Jeremiah 45:5 reads, "...seek them not: for, behold, I will bring evil upon all flesh, saith the Lord: but thy life will I give unto thee for a prey in all places whither thou goest" (KJV).

In summary, this miniature chapter of five verses packs a powerful punch. While the words are humbling, the message is simple, and the path is clear. True success should not be measured by our worldly gain or attained with a selfish heart. After all, we are not here for the world to see us... we are here for the world to see HIM!

Whatever the next phase of my life holds, it's not about me. It's about HIM.

My purpose in life... *it's beyond me.*

BIBLE READING: JEREMIAH 45

The Next Rainbow

"THESE THINGS I HAVE SPOKEN UNTO YOU, THAT IN ME YE MIGHT HAVE PEACE. IN THE WORLD YE SHALL HAVE TRIBULATION: BUT BE OF GOOD CHEER; I HAVE OVERCOME THE WORLD." JOHN 16:33 KJV

Up, up, up. The ascent is torturous. I squeeze my eyes closed and hold on so tight that my knuckles are white. On top of that, I am in physical pain from the lap bar. When the attendant instructed the riders to push the bar down until it clicked, I wanted to be sure, so I sucked in and got an extra click. Now, I am pretty sure it is rubbing against my spine. The voices of my family prodding at me echo in the background. They like to play a game to see who can get me to open my eyes, but right now, my thoughts are on what is to come. With every creak of the coaster being pulled to the top, the anxiety intensifies because I know once the little car reaches the peak, it is down, down, down, and that sharp pang will flow through my chest plunging my heart into my stomach. *Why is this supposed to be fun?*

I know this is not the first time I have referred to my fear of roller coasters. But, the phobia is so traumatizing that I feel the need to mention it again. Actually, I detest any amusement park ride that involves a sudden drop. My fear is so overwhelming that I cannot even stay calm when the coaster car is barely creeping up the incline... because I know what is coming when I get to the top. I am going DOWN.

However, when I think about it, roller coasters are not the only thing that spurs this same reaction. When great things are happening and life seems to be smooth sailing, I know I should be basking in the moment. But instead of enjoying the view from the mountaintop, I enter panic mode anticipating the fiery arrow that is going to send me spiraling from the picturesque summit into a valley of darkness.

Christians are not exempt from problems and hardships in life. Actually, the Bible tells us we will have struggles, but the Bible also tells us that, as Christians, God is with us through those struggles. John 16:33 says, "These things I have spoken unto you, that in me ye might have peace. In the world ye shall have tribulation: but be of good cheer; I have overcome the world" (KJV). Not only does the scripture say we will have tribulation, but the Bible is filled with stories of people facing struggles.

As a child, one of my favorite Bible stories was Noah's Ark because I loved animals and the bright colors of the rainbow. I can still see the image in my mind as I would hear the story. A giant wooden boat with a long string of animals lined up two by two as far as the eye can see. Noah with a tall cane in his hand stands beside the door keeping order as the animals walk up the ramp and board the ark. I did not think about the time frame and the amount of physical labor that went into constructing a ship of the magnitude of the ark. I did not think about the storm Noah and his family weathered inside of the ship being tossed about on waves with no land in sight. I did not think about how long a year would have seemed to Noah and his family enclosed in the ark. *Talk about going stir-crazy.* But, in the end, the sun came out.

I have heard the saying that it takes both the sun and the rain to make a rainbow. God placed the rainbow in the sky as a symbol of his promise to never destroy the earth by flood again. But when I see a rainbow, I am also reminded that if I keep my trust in God, He will see me through the storm and let the sun's rays shine on me again. Just like a plant needs the rain and the sun to grow, so do we.

So, I want to end with a poem I wrote in one of my valleys. And I hope that when it storms... you remember the rainbow.

I stand with my shoulders slumped,
my body crumpling beneath the pounding rain.
My insides scream that I cannot
endure the pain.

It seems just yesterday I stood with full lungs
on the mountaintop,
the sun illuminated every space.
Happiness consumed me in the depths of my
soul,
and I had a smile that I thought could never be
erased.

Now, I have awakened in this valley of dark shadows hovering and smothering,
trying to steal every breath of air.
The enemy claws and rips at the wound telling
me to give up,
but a powerful voice says, "Just follow me, I will
help you escape this dragon's lair."

I hold on as He pulls me along,
and as the shadows fade, the sky gets a little
lighter.
The higher He pulls me, the higher we climb,
and the colors of the rainbow get a little brighter.

With every step, His hand squeezes mine,
and He whispers, "Take one more....
This is the only way to the mountain
that is better than the one before."

And then I remember as the rainbow comes into
full view,
the creator of this rainbow is also the creator of
me.

With every valley that I endure,
and every new rainbow that I see,

if I keep my faith and trust in Him,
through the smiles and tears, through the agony
and glee,
my Father will lead me to the mountaintop
with the golden plans designed especially for me.

BIBLE READING: JOHN 16:33

Notes

_____
_____
_____
_____
_____
_____
_____
_____
_____
_____
_____
_____
_____
_____
_____
_____
_____

Notes

Notes

Notes

Sharpening Our Sword

Over the past year, I have set a goal to sharpen my sword by memorizing a Bible verse each week. In doing so, I write the verse in my journal at the beginning of the week and recite it aloud each morning. I invite you to join me on this journey. Use the following pages to record a verse to memorize each week of the coming uear... and let's sharpen our sword together.

1._____
_____
_____
2._____
_____
_____
3._____
_____
_____
4._____
_____
_____
5._____
_____
_____
6._____
_____
_____
7._____
_____
_____

8._____

_____

_____

9._____

_____

_____

10._____

_____

_____

11._____

_____

_____

12._____

_____

_____

13._____

_____

_____

14._____

_____

_____

15._____
_____
_____

16._____
_____
_____

17._____
_____
_____

18._____
_____
_____

19._____
_____
_____

20._____
_____
_____

21._____
_____
_____

22._____

_____

23._____

_____

24._____

_____

25._____

_____

26._____

_____

27._____

_____

28._____

_____

_____

29._____

_____

_____

30._____

_____

_____

31._____

_____

32._____

_____

33._____

_____

_____

34._____

_____

_____

35._____

_____

36. _____

_____

_____

37. _____

_____

_____

38. _____

_____

_____

39. _____

_____

_____

40. _____

_____

_____

41. _____

_____

_____

42. _____

_____

_____

43._____

_____

44._____

_____

45._____

_____

46._____

_____

47._____

_____

48._____

_____

49._____

_____

_____

50._____
_____
_____
51._____
_____
_____
52._____
_____
_____

Acknowledgements

All praise and glory goes to the Heavenly Father, for without Him, I could do nothing.

I want to thank my husband and children for always being there to encourage me and boost my confidence and for loving me unconditionally, my mother for her endless hours of proofreading and being there to help me no matter what, my Warrior Sister for lifting me daily and helping me hold my shield, my mother-in-law for encouraging me and loving me as her own, and last but certainly not least, all who have read my books, left reviews, and follow my progress in my newsletter and social media, I appreciate you more than you will ever know.

About the Author

F. D. ADKINS

F. D. Adkins is a Christian fiction author and freelance writer. She hopes to pass along the comfort that comes from having a personal relationship with Jesus while offering her readers a brief escape from life's struggles through an action-packed story full of suspense, twists, turns, love, and a few laughs. In other words, her passion is sharing her faith through fiction.

She currently has three Christian Suspense Thriller novels, *TRUTH IN THE NAME*, *TRUTH IN THE WORD*, and *NEVER FORGET THE TRUTH*. In 2023, *TRUTH IN THE NAME* received third place in the Selah Awards in the category of 'First Novel' and recently won the 2024American Legacy Book Award in the 'Thriller: Religious' category. She has had freelance articles published in *FOCUS ON*

THE FAMILY magazine and *FAITH ON EVERY COR-NER* magazine. In addition, F. D. Adkins posts every Monday to a faith blog on her website.

She has been married to the man of her dreams and her best friend for 25 years. She loves spending time with her family, reading, and writing and always enjoys a good cup of coffee. She also has a soft spot in her heart for all animals, especially dogs.

She lives in South Carolina with her husband, Steve, their two children, Landon and Layna, and their dog, Lucy.

Check out this Christian Suspense Thriller series by F. D. Adkins

The **TRUTH** Trilogy

A thought-provoking journey that challenges the limits of human perception and cuts to the very essence of what it means to know God.

**What if someone erased your memory?
Would you still know God?**

**If the enemy came to lay his claim,
would you bear the seal of the HOLIEST NAME?**

**When the forces of darkness masquerade in the light,
is your sword sharpened in TRUTH and wielded to fight?**

In Memory Of

Dorothy Costner
&
Charles Adkins

I am so thankful for your legacy of faith. Your love for Jesus will forever be etched in my mind and held close to my heart.

Made in the USA
Columbia, SC
03 December 2024

48395051R00169